THE JOY OF CAMPING

PHOEBE SMITH

summersdale

THE JOY OF CAMPING

Summersdale Publishers Ltd
46 West Street
Chichester
West Sussex
PO19 1RP
UK

www.summersdale.com

Printed and bound in the Czech Republic

ISBN: 978-1-84953-698-1

Substantial discounts on bulk quantities of Summersdale books are available to corporations, professional associations and other organisations. For details contact Nicky Douglas by telephone: +44 (0) 1243 756902, fax: +44 (0) 1243 786300 or email: nicky@summersdale.com.

*In memory of Georgina Smith and
Michael Price for all the joy they brought
everyone lucky enough to have met them*

CONTENTS

INTRODUCTION

*'It is surprising with what impunity and comfort one who
has always lain in a warm bed in a close apartment, and
studiously avoided drafts of air, can lie down on the ground
without a shelter, roll himself in a blanket, and sleep before
a fire, in a frosty autumn night, just after a long rain-storm,
and even come soon to enjoy and value the fresh air.'*

HENRY DAVID THOREAU

From building a fort in our living room made of sofa cushions and a
bedspread, to pitching a tent in our own back garden or maybe even
being forced into a rainy family holiday under canvas – camping, in
some form or other, is something we all seem to be introduced to
fairly early on in our lives.

For many, that initiation into a world
of Trangias, sleeping bags and
ice-cold trips to the toilet
block is something we first
experience as a child on
family holidays. The
campsites we go to

become the places where very first adventures are had, friends are made and lasting memories created. For many, that's where it ends – as something left firmly in the past. Something to laugh about from inside our cosy centrally-heated houses and then think, 'Why did we ever do that?' But, for the rest of us, those trips sparked something within us. A love for bedding down outside. For us, camping is addictive.

We don't mind sleeping with a hat on, or waking up with a cold nose. It worries us not that we are kept awake with the rhythmic spitter-spatter of raindrops drumming against our tent walls. We, proudly, are campers and we know something that all those brick-building dwellers do not: that these are the times of our lives.

People are different on campsites. There, without four walls to contain us, we smile a little easier, we help each other a little more willingly and we begin to realise that there's more entertainment in a campfire than anything to be found on the internet; more excitement in sleeping with nothing more than a zip between us and the wildlife outside, rather than in seeing it on TV; more sense of satisfaction in erecting our own shelter than in paying someone else to do it for us; more magic in a sunset than money could ever buy – and more exhilaration found in waking up to fresh air and natural views than we can ever really explain.

It's not that we ignore the negatives we face when camping – the cold nights, the damp mornings, the noisy neighbours, the sheer refusal of a tent to fit back inside the same bag it came in – but we're so content to be out there, breathing in fresh air amid spectacular surrounds and like-minded people, that they just don't bother us.

There are a great many more things we could do with our precious free time than camp – as we're used to people telling us frequently. We could stay in five-star hotels, indulging in spa treatments and fluffy duvets with gourmet food served on tap. We could simply buy a conveniently pre-arranged package holiday where all we need is contained in our resort – along with group activities and on-hand excursions. We could simply stay at home and do nothing, enjoying a lazy time of it in the warmth of our own bed.

So why *do* we do it? Perhaps it's the camaraderie of the campsite. It could be the simplicity of making do without all the so-called luxuries we've been convinced we can't live without. Or maybe it's because pitching our tent allows us to feel like children again, building a temporary den on a little patch of wilderness where, outside the door, anything could happen…

THE HISTORY OF CAMPING

*'Thousands of tired, nerve-shaken, over-civilized people
are beginning to find out going to the mountains is
going home; that wilderness is a necessity…'*

JOHN MUIR

With quirky designs coming out every year, tons of accessories available and shops devoted entirely to the activity, it would be easy to believe that camping was a fairly recent invention – something done only for fun rather than necessity – but it's not. Don't forget that ever since humans have existed on earth, we have dedicated our time to finding some kind of shelter in which we can sleep safety.

From our hunter-gatherer ancestors who made structures among the trees and caves, to the nomadic tribes who would pack up their self-built communities and move according both to the seasons and the prey, we have always been on a quest to create warm, dry and comfortable sleeping compartments.

All that culminated in the creation of one key camping 'must have' – the tent. Though no one can trace exactly which type of tent came first, among the earliest were teepees (North America), lavvu (The Arctic) and yurts (Asia). Though slightly different in shape and structure – either pyramids or bell-shaped – all had the same properties in common: the ability to be taken apart, moved and rebuilt somewhere else. Those same designs were adopted when tents began to be mass-produced for military purposes – replacing wooden poles for metal, and animal hide for canvas. The technology may have changed, but tents were still used and designed for more utilitarian purposes rather than pleasure. That was until 1853, when a young man who had travelled across the prairies of North America with his family – sleeping in a wagon en route – arrived back in Britain.

Thomas Hiram Holding yearned for the kind of experiences he remembered from his childhood: that endless, exciting movement, and the ability to call anywhere home when you could take that home with you. So he started to undertake a series of adventures.

First he headed to Scotland with his canoe and tent and travelled around the Highlands on a mini-expedition. Next, as cycling was his passion, he persuaded a group of friends to accompany him as he journeyed to Connemara, Ireland, for a few weeks of pedalling and sleeping out under the stars. This 'cycle camping', as he called it, enthralled him so much that in 1901 he formed the Association of Cycle Campers.

That was only the beginning. A tailor by trade, he combined his knack for design with his pastime and began experimenting with tent structures. Using oiled silk and bamboo poles – which he even fashioned to be telescopic – he is credited as being one of the early pioneers of lightweight shelters. And it didn't stop there. He also created a portable stove and then wrote a book called *The Camper's Handbook* (printed in 1908), which was one of the first books in Britain to detail 'how to' and 'where to' information about tent sleeping in the UK.

From small beginnings, his club continued to grow and flourish, extending on many years after Holding passed away. Wondering what became of the Cycle Campers? Well now they go by a different name – The Camping and Caravanning Club, which not only has in excess of 800 sites and 400,000 members, but also offers pitches overseas too. Not bad for a project that began with only passion to fuel it…

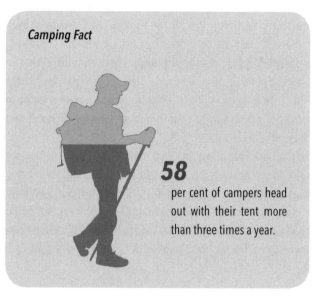

Camping Fact

58 per cent of campers head out with their tent more than three times a year.

(Go Outdoors Camping Survey, 2014)

How did camping get so popular?

In a strange and unexpected twist of fate, the advent of World War One had, perhaps, the biggest impact on camping. Though people like Thomas Hiram Holding had already begun to do it for fun pre-1914, and many climbers had been camping for years before that in order to stay close to the crags they wanted to ascend, it wasn't until serving soldiers returned from the trenches that the hobby really started to become popular among the masses.

It's logical if you really think about it. The conditions in the trenches were very basic, but being stuck in them for four years made people realise that they could get by without any mod cons or home comforts. The war forced people to travel to fight for King and Country and, for many working-class men, the first time they had seen the world had been from within the walls of a tent. Therefore returning to the luxury of home and staying in one place would have felt very strange for some, and so they would have looked to the outdoors for a sense of freedom and familiarity. Add to that the quantity and cheapness of army surplus kit that suddenly flooded the post-war market, as well as the increase in people buying their own vehicles rather than using trains, and it's not surprising that the years that followed the Great War saw more and more people heading to the Great Outdoors with their families on camping trips.

In 1932, camping had become so popular that The Camping and Caravanning Club formed the International Federation of Camping Clubs (Fédération Internationale de Camping et de Caravanning, FICC). This meant that other national camping clubs worldwide were affiliated with them, creating a global network of opportunities to camp out.

Though an understandable dip in spending time under canvas happened during the late thirties and early forties, people were still eager to escape the cities and, once World War Two ended in 1945, people picked up where they left off, and tent-based holidays became popular once more.

Top ten reasons why camping is great

 You get to wake up without an alarm clock. Surrounded by natural light, you rise when the sun does and it's perfectly acceptable to go to bed when it gets dark – meaning many more hours in bed than you'd normally get at home, so you wake up feeling refreshed.

 Sleeping bags. There's no scientific reason to explain this, but why is it that snuggling down in a sleeping bag is so much cosier than a duvet?

 Pubs are always close by. Good campsites are always close to great pubs, which means you can spend the day walking or having outdoor adventures, reward yourself with a pint and a hot pub meal, then curl up inside your well-deserved sleeping bag (see above).

 Visitors of the wild variety may drop by. Sleeping in the outdoors means wildlife will literally be on your doorstop. From rabbits to foxes, birds to bats, you'll always have guaranteed 'wild nights out' when camping.

You have an excuse to leave Facebook/ Twitter/the phone at home . Embrace the fact that some campsites are off-grid and that camping will give you a chance to reconnect with the natural world, so set your Facebook status to 'completely happy' and enjoy!

 Stars will always beat any ceiling. It's amazing how a night spent gazing at the blanket of constellations up above can remind us just how big the world is, and how lucky we are to be a part of it.

 It's cheap. Once you've made the initial outlay of buying your kit, you suddenly have the chance to sleep in some of the best places in the world for the smallest price tags.

 It can be as mild or as wild as you'd like. Just because you are outdoors doesn't mean you have to be Bear Grylls. If you want to bring everything and a kitchen sink – do it. Equally, if you want to go superlight and wild camp in the hills – do it. The choice is always yours.

You start to realise that the best things in life aren't 'things' – when you're watching that sunset without intently using your smartphone, watching TV or having anything else distract you, you'll begin to talk to your family or friends, or simply start to take in the wonderful world around you.

You'll meet like-minded people – socialising with fellow campers is what it's all about, from conversations on the latest tent models to simply sharing a mallet to hammer your tent pegs in, camping will bring you together with some wonderful people.

Camping Fact

In the 1930s, the establishment worried that the increase in camping activity would mean that the countryside would fast become crowded with tent-carrying poor, so a number of Government bills were mocked up in an attempt to restrict it. Thankfully, it was not passed. (Source: www.campr.co.uk)

If they can do it...

Another activity that planted tent-based trips in the public's imagination was mountaineering. The race to be the first person to summit Mount Everest had been going on since its height was first officially published in the Great Trigonometrical Survey of India in 1856. So, predictably, by the time it actually did happen, nearly 100 years later in 1953, interest in expeditions to distant lands had reached fever pitch. When Hillary and Tenzing finally stepped foot on the summit of the highest mountain on earth, having tented their way to the top, camping's popularity soared.

In-tents changes

Enter the 1960s, and from that point on it wasn't just the idea of camping that had evolved – tents themselves changed. Gone was the dull and heavy khaki canvas. Now came the era of nylon and printed fabrics boasting bright colours and intended for families. Destinations also stretched further afield. The introduction of affordable flights and cheap package holidays meant that people were no longer confined to British shores. Camping went overseas, European-style, with people seeking guaranteed sun rather than risking a rainy escape in Britain.

Camping Fact

The most popular overseas camping destination with the British is France – with a whopping 61 per cent of campers choosing it as the place to pitch in 2014. Spain, Germany and Italy came in second, third and fourth, respectively.

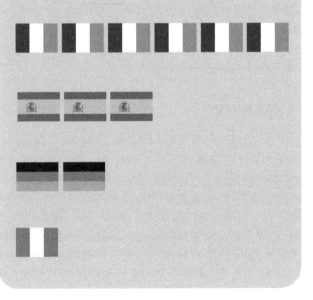

(Go Outdoors Camping Survey, 2014)

Top six reasons people camp

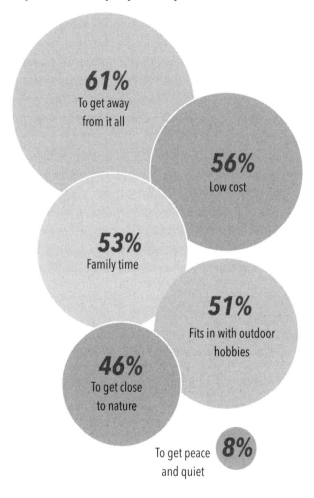

61%
To get away
from it all

56%
Low cost

53%
Family time

51%
Fits in with outdoor
hobbies

46%
To get close
to nature

8%

To get peace
and quiet

(Go Outdoors Camping Survey, 2014)

Every cloud...

With the advent of cheap 'package' travel abroad, where all-inclusive hotels were offered at low rates, camping could have been abandoned entirely except by all but the few outdoor aficionados – but it didn't end there. Due to a financial recession in the 1980s, going abroad suddenly became a luxury that not many could afford. Once again, the tent saw a resurgence and the public fell back in love with the budget option that camping offered.

The economy slowly recovered but yet another recession hit before the millennium and people gradually became more aware of their environmental impact on the planet, meaning they looked for more 'green' credentials in their recreational activities. Add the 2008 recession to the economic mix and it wasn't long before the now-famed word 'Staycation' hit the headlines, with increasing numbers of people searching for adventure in their own backyard – and on the cheap.

Camping Fact

One in three people took a camping or caravanning holiday in the UK between 2009 and 2011 – up from one in five before 2009. (Source: Mintel, 2011)

Camping Fact

1.2 million

The number of Brits who now choose camping
as their preferred holiday every year.

Introducing luxury

But it wasn't just budget-hunters that started the quest for nights out
in the great outdoors. Those who liked creature comforts also started
to yearn for a little excitement. So it's no surprise that, these days, tents
range from small, uber-lightweight one-person numbers to all-singing,
all-dancing, multi-roomed abodes that take a wood-burning stove.
Campsites vary from a simple field to all-out five-star plots, complete
with luxury bathrooms and electricity supplied to every pitch. And
accessories go from the simple foam sleeping mat to solar-powered
hair straighteners – with many more ludicrous inventions in between.

In 2010, the Office of National Statistics released figures that showed
5.43 million camping trips were made in 2009 – an increase of 29 per
cent year on year. For the first time on record, that number overtook
bed and breakfast stays (which were 4.98 million). Long live the tent!

Four health benefits of camping

1. Fresh air

   Studies have shown that our bodies benefit from extra oxygen found in the great outdoors – not only that, fresh air is also shown to lower blood pressure, help digestion and boost your immune system.

2. Sunlight

   The extra melatonin you get from the huge amounts of natural light you're exposed to as a camper has been shown to improve your mood, with campers consistently reporting feeling happier than non-campers.

3. No stress

   As many 'sights' are situated in remote areas, when we pitch camp we often find ourselves cut off , with no phone signal or Wi-Fi – but this gives us time to switch off and reconnect with nature, lowering stress levels that in the long-term can increase your lifespan.

4. Activity

   Even putting up a tent will get you moving and, as there's only so long most of us can sit still in a tent with the outdoors right on our doorstep (literally) most campers are by very nature more physically active. This improves the health of our heart and lungs.

One campsite in numbers: Cunningham Camp, Howstrake, Isle of Man

1894

The year this, the first known campsite in the British Isles, opened

600

The number of visitors who visited the above site each week during the season (May–October)

0

The number of female visitors who stayed (it was a 'Young Men's Holiday Camp')

8

The number of men who would share each one of the tents

5

Acres of land the campsite purchased in 1904 due to its increasing popularity

100

Feet, the length of the dining hall built to serve the keen campers

1,500

Tents were erected for the season

17/6

The amount in shillings and pence it cost to stay at the camp per week (about 90p in today's money)

1911

The year when a public meeting was held in the town hall to demand bye-laws were introduced at the site to stop 'alleged illegalities' – including prohibiting women to stay

1945

The year the site was sold to a Blackpool businessman, later becoming holiday accommodation

(www.isleofman.com)

CHAPTER 2

TENT TALK

'The canvas wanted more putting up than I think any of us had bargained for. You would not imagine this to be dangerous work but, looking back now, the wonder is to me that any of us are alive to tell the tale...'

JEROME K. JEROME

Despite all the technical jargon, and the list of names and styles, strip a tent bare and beneath it all they are all the same: a mix of poles, guy-lines and inner and outer sheets. But what bit goes where? And how can you erect one without getting fed up and having a domestic on the campsite? Never fear, help is at hand, because after this chapter you too, will sound like a pro in the world of tent talk.

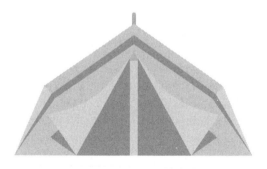

Deconstructing tents

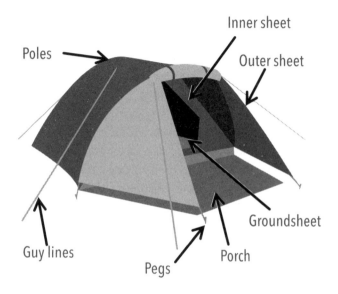

Inner sheet

Outer sheet

Poles

Groundsheet

Guy lines

Porch

Pegs

Inner sheet – To keep you dry, tents are made up of two layers: the inner sheet that makes up the walls of your tent when you are inside it, and the outer sheet (also known as the flysheet). Even without the outer sheet, the inner is a complete structure with a zippable door which, in good quality models, is fitted with a midge net to stop bugs getting in but still allowing air to circulate. If staying somewhere hot and if you're sure it won't rain, then you can easily get away with sleeping inside an inner sheet only.

Outer sheet – This goes over the top of the inner sheet and will be the part that also forms a porch at the entrance. It's a waterproof layer, so when camping somewhere wet you need to use this. After long use (every couple of years on average, but more frequently if you use it a lot) you will need to re-proof it with a special spray (available in most camping stores) to keep the rain out. The key thing you need to remember when pitching is that the inner and outer sheets should be kept taut so that they do not touch each other. If they do, then you won't get enough air circulating in between the layers, and so the inner tent walls will become saturated with condensation.

Some tents pitch inner first, forming the basic structure. Then the outer sheet goes over the top. Others pitch outer first and then you get inside to pitch the inner next, clipping it to the outer. The latter is best if you're likely to camp in rainy conditions as you can finish putting up the tent without getting wet. Some models even come with the inner and outer already connected so you pitch it all in one.

Groundsheet – This is the part of the tent that you lie on, and is usually made from a more robust waterproof fabric than the rest of the structure, as this is what separates you from the ground. Usually, this is stitched on to the rest of the inner tent, and a good one will rise up the sides by several inches. In teepees or larger family tents these are sometimes separate and attach to the main structure of the tent using a series of clips or hooks.

Guy lines – These are the cords that you peg in to the ground after you've secured the outer sheet. They work to keep the tent stable in high winds and keep the outer sheet taut so it doesn't sag and touch the inner sheet.

Pegs – Much like tents, these come in a range of shapes and sizes. Lighter ones reduce your pack weight, but if they're just thin wire needles they won't be useful on rocky ground or hard soil. More heavy duty ones will withstand strong wind better and are needed for larger tent structures. Some are plastic, most are metal and these days you can even get re-usable biodegradable ones which, if left by mistake, will begin to break down into the ground, leaving no trace. No matter which ones come with the tent you buy, don't forget that you can always replace them with a different set that will suit your camping needs.

Poles – These are vital to form the structure and shape of the tent. Normally made of alloy, they have shock cords running through them so you can dismantle them and fold them up to fit in the stuff sack. Depending on the style of the tent, they fit in sleeves on either the outer or inner sheet and lock into eyelets to keep them in place.

Porch – A great place for cooking in high winds or storing dirty boots and wet gear, the porch is sheltered from the elements as it's under the flysheet, but outside the inner tent. It always has a door on it that can be folded back and secured. It won't have a groundsheet in it so remember that anything you place here will get wet.

Camping Fact

In 1973, Hilleberg made the first commercial tent to have connected inner and outer sheets. This meant that, for the first time, you could pitch both the inner and outer in one go.

Tent technology

From humble beginnings…

The earliest shelters, and therefore tents, were constructed with whatever humans could find. Poles were wooden at first and the outer and inner sheets were a mixture of animal hide and vegetation, i.e. leaves and branches. These worked well, but certainly weren't the most lightweight option.

With innovations in fabric towards the end of the nineteenth century, the earliest man-made tents tended to be produced using 100 per cent cotton canvas. Indeed, in 1875, one of the oldest tent manufacturers in the USA – Armbruster Manufacturers, responsible for supplying tents to troops in World War One and Two – used canvas to mass produce these heavy duty shelters.

As it naturally breathes, canvas is perfect for keeping the interior of a tent cool when it's hot and warm when it's cold. Also, after being wet a couple of times, the fibres move together – making the structure waterproof. As it has these natural ventilation properties it actually would be one of the best fabrics for sleeping in, as it doesn't get the build-up of condensation that more modern fabrics do. However, it has one major disadvantage – weight.

Though these structures were fine in a military environment when durability was of utmost importance, today's backpackers want a tent to be mobile and easy to carry in a rucksack. You can still see some canvas-style tents on campsites today, but these tend to be bell tents or yurts, designed to stay in one place (e.g. for 'glamping'), and so negating the need for a lighter weight.

Moving things on a little... extra durability and waterproofability was achieved by the addition of a PVC (Polyvinyl Chloride) coating to traditional canvas in the 1960s – mainly around the tent roof area. These kinds of tents can still be seen today, though due to their heavier weight and bulk they are, more often than not, used only as awnings to camper vans or for the production of marquees.

Lighten up

As with clothing fabric, 100 per cent cotton went out of fashion after World War Two and was replaced with a blend of natural and man-made materials. Combining cotton with polyester meant reducing the weight but didn't compromise on robustness, and so was a popular choice among campers. However, these tents did have to be coated to make them waterproof as they lost the naturally occurring properties of pure cotton.

In an attempt to make things lighter still, manufacturers dispensed with cotton altogether and started to experiment with fabric that could work like cotton. Polyester was a popular choice, as was nylon. The main advantage of polyester is that it doesn't go slack and baggy even when very wet, and won't be damaged by UV in the same way as nylon (nylon needs to be treated, as prolonged exposure to the sun will render its waterproofing less effective). Both materials are still used in tents today, from the incredibly cheap to the ludicrously expensive.

It's all about the coating

So what is it that separates the budget models from the expedition variety? It's all about the coating. As with anything, from acrylic (cheaper but not as effective or long-lasting) to polyurethane (more durable) and silicone (super lightweight, super effective and longer-lasting but very expensive), you do get what you pay for.

Tent tip

Whichever tent you get, make sure you look after it to prolong its lifespan. Don't pack it away after each trip without first drying it out thoroughly and cleaning it. Also consider buying re-proofer and UV protection sprays and regularly treat it with this to make it last.

Pole position

Of course it wasn't just fabrics that evolved. Poles changed from wood to metal - specifically steel and aluminium. They can be rigid, as found in larger tents, or bendy as in most backpacking and lightweight models. Rigid ones are normally steel, and coated to stop rusting, whereas aluminium - which is naturally less corrosive - will probably be polished. Many of the superlight tent poles - for tunnels and domes - are made from fibreglass (sometimes coated, sometimes not). This makes them easy to erect and they do stand up to bad weather well, bouncing back and forth in high winds to avoid breaking - just *don't* step on one as they're fragile! Most should have an elastic cord that runs through and connects them all up to make things easier.

Easy pitch

Enter the millennium and we started to see a new style of tent hitting the shelves – the pop-up tent. These hooped-shaped packages could be easily unzipped to reveal a tent that literally pitched itself in seconds – all you had to do was peg it down to stop it blowing away in the wind. These were instantly popular with festival-goers and children – as well as new campers. The main problem is that they are tricky to get back into their bags! Though not impossible, seeing a frustrated couple arguing over the best way to do this was a frequent sight on the campground in the late 2000s! Another drawback, of course, is that they don't pack down small like a traditional tent with collapsible poles.

Did you know…?

The Guinness World Record Holder for the lightest tent is held by British Company, Terra Nova. Based in Derbyshire, their Laser Ultra 1 hits the scales at just 580 g (that's a smidgen more than the iPad!).

Hot air

At present, the latest style in tents is the 'inflatables'. Not the whole thing you understand… just the poles. All the tent fabric and poles are stitched together as a complete structure, and you just pump air into the 'pole' sections (actually stitched cylinders) and *voila* – the whole thing is erect! Easy to put up (perhaps a little harder to deflate), these tents usually come with a pump which you attach to the beams. Get going and your tent – even a large family-size model – can be up in three minutes. Stronger than you might think, they make an impressively rigid and durable structure. They are also built with isolation valves to stop the whole thing coming down if it gets a puncture. Better yet, all the elements of the tent are attached already – outer and inner sheets plus groundsheet – so it really does get top marks for ease of use. The pump will add extra weight but there's no way you'd want to improvise with lung power – it would take hours. As with most things, this simplicity of construction comes with a much higher price tag. But for campsite ease, it's no wonder that these models are becomes increasingly popular fixtures on sites.

Things to ask yourself before you buy a tent

Taking the plunge and buying a new shelter? Consider these questions before you buy…

1. How many people do I need it for?

Tents come in various sizes. If you plan on going solo, then a one-person model will be fine. Likewise, if you're a couple, a two-person version will do the job. But if you plan to go regularly with friends, or take the kids, you should consider getting one slightly bigger than the number of people you'll be sharing with so you won't be treading on each other's toes. Family tents tend to have separate sleeping quarters offering some amount of privacy… just remember that tents are not soundproof!

2. Will you be car camping or backpacking?

Transporting a tent is definitely something to think about now. If you only plan to sleep in official campsites with all the facilities and keep your car alongside you the whole time, then size and weight cease to matter. But if you plan on multi-day backpacking trips, sleeping out in the wild, or want to walk between different campsites on a long-distance trek, then every gram will count; go for a lighter-weight model.

3. What style would you prefer?

This is very much a personal choice. The main ones available to you will be:

Tunnel tents - Often the lightest designs, these are usually made of one, two or three central hoops only. They rely on traction to create a tunnel shape, which you make yourself when pegging it out. You tend to get a good amount of space inside with this design. However, you will need to be efficient at getting them taut so they don't sag in the middle and the inner and outer sheets don't touch.

Geodesic - Invented after World War One and also known as dome tents, their main feature is that, once the poles are in place, the tent is freestanding. This means you can move it once it's up if you find the ground is bumpy and then simply peg it in place to hold it down. The downside? It can be a slightly heavier option compared to tunnel tents.

Box tents – The design that most large family tents are based on, they offer an abundance of headroom, which means you can stand up and walk around in them as if at home. They usually have several 'rooms', but because of this feature they are heavy and often a little more complicated to erect.

And now for something a little different…

The A-frame – It looks nice and nostalgic, but with sloping sides that meet at the top creating a triangular shape, the amount of internal space is limited compared to other models.

Conical tents – Think yurt, teepee and lavvu. These tents are formed using a single, central pole that allows shelter to be created quickly. The cone shape means a low centre of gravity, which keeps the tent stable in the wind and leaves plenty of space in the centre (originally used for a wood-burning stove or fire).

CHAPTER 3

CAMPING ESSENTIALS

*'There's no such thing as bad weather,
only inappropriate clothing.'*
SIR RANULPH FIENNES

Visit a camping shop today and it's very easy to be put off. With a whole host of brands and fabrics all vying for your attention and screaming 'buy me!' it's hard to work out what you need as opposed to what you don't. No one wants to waste money on something they'll never use, and camping is supposed to be about getting back to nature (not pretending you're actually not part of it), so while creature comforts are good, let's strip it down to the absolute basics of what you really need.

Sleeping

Sleeping mat - You need something to insulate you from the ground - it will get cold, even in summer. There are lots of options available - from a heavy, but supremely comfortable, flocked mattress or metal-framed camp bed (car camping only; remember the pump if required!) to a self-inflating lightweight number or traditional closed-cell foam mat. The latter is the cheapest, but can be bulky and not as comfortable.

Sleeping bag - Filled with down (from ducks or geese) or synthetic material (man-made fibres), the choice is yours. Down can be lighter for the same level of warmth as some heavier synthetics, but if you get it wet/damp it won't work properly. So think carefully about the conditions you'll experience. Check the temperature ratings when buying to make sure you'll stay warm enough. The key thing is to get a product that offers maximum warmth to weight ratio. Manufacturers print a range of temperatures on their bags - look for the comfort rating, as this is the most useful. Consider taking an inflatable pillow for maximum comfort (or you could roll up an insulated jacket instead).

Accessories

*'She had the loaded handbag of someone who camps out…
or who imagines life must be full of emergencies.'*

Mavis Gallant

Don't go overboard here (easier said than done!). In a world where there's seemingly a gadget for every eventuality, remember that often, less is more. Here's what you really need:

Head torch - From finding your belongings in a bag, to finding your way to the toilet block in the campsite, you need some form of light. Normal torches or special camping lanterns will do the job in a larger tent. But, to keep your hands free when cooking or reading, you can't beat a head torch. Look for one with different beam intensity settings, which is adjustable, and sits comfortably on your head.

Antibacterial gel - Great for keeping things clean and you don't need a towel or water to use it.

Wash bag - Take a separate bag with your supplies in and don't get carried away - a simple toothbrush and paste and shower gel or soap will suffice.

Duct tape - A great accessory that fixes a multitude of sins - wrap it around your walking poles (if you take them). It takes up no room and will definitely come in handy to fix tent poles, ripped groundsheets and more.

Warm jacket – As the sun sets you will get colder, even if it's summer; make sure you take a warm jacket to put over your other clothes so you don't have to go straight to bed when the sun sets. Jackets come with either down or synthetic insulation. As with sleeping bags, down is excellent at giving warmth while remaining lightweight, but synthetic insulation will work better if wet. There is now 'hydrophobic' down on the market that does work better if damp; it's just a case of choosing your preference.

Rucksack – If you're wild camping/backpacking between campsites you'll need to make sure your rucksack is big enough for all your kit. A 45–50-litre bag is usually sufficient, being large enough but not unnecessarily big or unwieldy.

Tent, sweet tent...

Taking the basics with you will ensure your tent is comfortable enough, but how do you make it feel like a home from home? Here are a few extra tips you can try to make your tent feel more homely.

Dry bags (optional) – Often sold in packs of several different colours and sizes, these are a great way to organise your kit and keep anything important away from condensation.

Warm up – Consider taking a hot-water bottle. Getting into a pre-warmed sleeping bag is an experience that everyone should have. Sleep tight!

Put up a flag or some bunting - A great way to not only personalise your space and allow you to spot your tent in a crowded campsite, but also to create a talking point; it's a good way of making new friends easily!

Consider a 'carpet' - Whether you take a rug, a blanket or a tent 'footprint' for the porch, having something warm underfoot will make any tent feel instantly cosy.

 Take a pillow - You don't have to 'rough it' with a jacket rolled-up under your head! Bring an actual pillow and you'll immediately be transported back to your own comfy bed.

Light a lantern - Head torches are a must for camping - handy to see what you're doing and keeping your hands free - but you can't beat a lantern hanging from your tent. It makes the space feel like a proper room (and avoids the classic blinding-your-fellow-campers-with-a-head-torch fiasco!)

 Take a seat - Sitting crossed-legged on the floor is all well and good, but bringing a camping chair will be much better for your back long-term and take you off the cold floor when the sun sets.

Towel - Not necessarily needed but, if you do decide to take one, make it small and ensure that it's quick-drying. A microfibre towel is a good option as it is tiny and super-fast drying.

Cooking equipment

> *'Happiness flutters in the air whilst we rest*
> *among the breaths of nature.'*
>
> KELLY SCHEAFFER

No matter if you're staying at a campsite or bedding down in the wild, the heart of any campsite is the kitchen. Whether a traditional fire-pit, a barbecue or a simple stove, where there's food, there are people – and when there's *good* food, there are happy campers!

Cooking pot

Stove

Fuel

Utensils

Stove – The choices are growing all the time. From an up-market twin-hobbed propane number with added grilling capability, to a basic Kelly Kettle (a portable, lightweight metal, chimney design, powered by dry tinder and even dry animal dung!), there's a range of options. Single hobs are great for boiling water or making simple meals, whereas a twin hob will enable you to do something more complicated. By far the easiest is the very efficient Jetboil – which has its own pot built in and nestles into a cup/bowl. Remember to take matches or a lighter.

Fuel – Where there's a stove you need fire, so make sure you bring the right fuel for your cooking system. Most require a simple gas cylinder, which is usually formed from a butane/propane mix and is available in small sizes for backpacking and in larger canisters for campsite use. Check that your stove has an igniter built in. If not (or just as a back-up) make sure you remember to take a lighter or box of matches. If opting for a barbecue, make sure you remember the charcoal and firelighters/lighting paper.

Cooking pot/mess tin (if not built into stove) – For heating food and water. Make sure it comes with a handle, or take an oven mitt to help with handling this item.

Utensils – Take enough cutlery, plates/bowls and mugs for all those in your party. A 'spork' (spoon, knife and fork combination) is useful for eating.

Your campsite kitchen

While you obviously can't – and shouldn't – take everything plus the kitchen sink with you, it doesn't mean that you have to compromise on great meals. It's all about packing the right gear.

For cooking ease, remember to bring:

Frying pan
Saucepan
Wooden spoon
Tongs
Sharp knife
Chopping board
Scissors
Bottle/can opener
Water container – you don't want to keep going back and forth to the tap every time you need H_2O, so take a large container with you.

What shall I cook?

With the right kit you can go elaborate if you want. But it's good to have a couple of mainstay basic camping recipes up your sleeve – nice and portable, even to take with you on a wild camp.

Campfire pizza

You might want to pre-mix some of this before you leave home, but you can easily cook a pizza on a camping stove... Just don't forget the frying pan.

Ingredients
3 tsp olive oil
200 g self-raising flour
Tube of passata (tomato paste)
1 fresh tomato, chopped
40 g cheese, grated

Method
1. Oil your frying pan then add the passata and the chopped tomato. Cook on a low heat for approximately 7 minutes, adding any spices or pepper/garnishes as preferred. Remove from heat.
2. In a bowl (or before you leave home) mix the flour with a teaspoon of olive oil and 5 tsp of water to form dough.
3. Roll out the dough into your pizza base shape, making sure it's not too big for the frying pan – if too big, cut to fit.
4. Add oil to the pan then place your pizza base inside and cook for about 10 minutes.
5. Get your tomato mix and spread on the pizza base. Add the cheese and cook for a further couple of minutes until the cheese melts and the base is fully cooked.
6. Serve and enjoy!

One-pan full English
Make a complete breakfast in a single pan so there's less washing-up at the campsite sink!

Ingredients (adjust to size of pan/party)
1 tbsp olive oil or a knob of butter
2 sausages (or veggie equivalent)
6 cherry tomatoes, halved
2 rashers of bacon (or veggie equivalent)
100 g mushrooms, chopped
4 eggs, beaten
Handful of grated cheese
Pinch of pepper

Method
1. Heat the pan. Add the butter or olive oil until it bubbles, then add the sausages. Cook for about 3–4 minutes, turning frequently.
2. Add the bacon, turning occasionally, then, once crisping up, throw in the mushrooms too. Cook for a further 5–6 minutes.
3. Add a pinch of pepper to the beaten eggs, then add to the pan, making sure you cover everything – omelette style. Add in the tomatoes and turn the heat down.
4. Leave for another couple of minutes, then add the cheese to the top. After about a minute, the cheese will have started to melt. Remove the whole thing from the flame and enjoy!

If you have a fire (or barbecue)

If an open flame or burning charcoals are on offer, seize the chance to make your camping meals much more hearty and your desserts more fun. Some fireside camping staples include:

Baked potato: Ah, the humble potato! You can't go wrong with one of these and even the culinary challenged can manage it. Simply wash, pierce with a fork several times, wrap in foil and then throw onto the coals or into the fire, and an hour later you'll have a tasty spud to replace lost carbs.

Corn on the cob: Another quick and easy snack. Simply wash, wrap in foil and let the flames do the rest. Should take around 10–15 minutes. Just don't forget the skewers, or prepare for burned fingers…

Bananas: A tasty sweet snack, yes, but pop them on the barbeque - no peeling required - and soon this warmed fruit becomes a savoury snack.

Marshmallows: An absolute classic. Simply find a stick, put a marshmallow on the end and place over the heat - soon a gooey treat will await. Best served with a good ghost story or a cheesy guitar rendition of 'Kumbaya'.

Food to go...

Heading out to camp in the wild? No room for a full-on campsite kitchen? Not to worry – food is in the bag…

Dehydrated – Packaged in a lightweight pouch, this is dried food that you simply add boiling water to and leave for several minutes before digging in (don't forget to remove the freshness crystal sachet before adding the water!). It's definitely the lightest option but a warning: if your stove doesn't work, or you can't source water, you will go hungry.

Pre-cooked – A heavier option, but in this packet all the food is already cooked so it simply needs heating up – boil-in-the-bag style. The advantage is that, in an emergency, you can resort to eating the contents cold. Yum!

It doesn't have to be dull

Pre-packed camping meals have a bad reputation: flavourless, too salty, too watery – there's just no pleasing some. But it doesn't have to be that way. Get some basics packed in your rucksack and you can add a definite *zing* to a meal. From extras like olives and sultanas to spices like coriander and oregano, or even baked beans or vegetable/meat stock, there's always a way to make them more appealing.

Wild food

Feeling hungry and want to try your hand at foraging? Here are a few handy extras to look out for in the great outdoors…

> Note, some fungi and plants can be poisonous – if in doubt, do not risk eating it!

 Wild garlic – Often found in ancient woodland, this can be identified by its clusters of white flowers and long, spear-shaped leaves. You'll be struck by a strong garlicky aroma when you've found them. You can chop up the leaves and flowers and add them to salads and soup or sauces, or, for something a bit special, brush bread with olive oil and toast, then finely chop the leaves and sprinkle them on the top.

Conifer needles – The green, pointy needles from pine or fir trees contain vitamin C and can be boiled to make a tea; go for the lighter-coloured ones for a less bitter taste.

 Blackberries – Found alongside many roads, canals and in woodland (usually between June and November) Make sure that you wash them well before you eat them. Good to throw into porridge to spice up your breakfast.

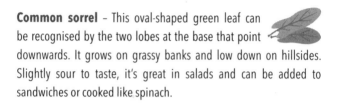

Common sorrel – This oval-shaped green leaf can be recognised by the two lobes at the base that point downwards. It grows on grassy banks and low down on hillsides. Slightly sour to taste, it's great in salads and can be added to sandwiches or cooked like spinach.

Dandelion – Not just an annoying weed in the garden, the dandelion can also be eaten – both flowers and leaves. Add them to salads or brew them up as a hot drink.

Fennel – For a quick burst of flavour and a spicy tang to your cooking, look for fennel. Identified by fleshy stems and a spray of lacelike yellow flowers, if you squash the stem and smell liquorice, then you've found it. Chop and add as seasoning.

Keeping things cool and secure

Remember that, as night falls, the temperature will drop, so the best way to keep items like milk cool is to leave them in the boot of your car (this also keeps any nosy wildlife out of it!)

If you've just boiled water to purify it and need to quickly cool it, try placing the container in a nearby stream. After a few minutes the temperature will have dropped significantly. Just remember to wedge it firmly between stones so that it doesn't get swept away with the current.

And that puts camping – quite literally – in the bag!

CHAPTER 4

PITCHER PERFECT

'What I like about camping is you can get really dirty. Either you're all by yourself, so no one else sees you, or everyone you're with is just as dirty as you are, so nobody cares.'

ANONYMOUS FORMER BOY SCOUT

So you've chosen your tent, got your bags packed, sorted the ingredients for the camping meal, remembered the fuel and have the campsite lingo down. Now all that's left to do is to rock up to your destination and pitch! Here are some tips for a good night's sleep…

Campsite conundrums

If you're not planning to go wild, and are opting for a good old-fashioned site complete with toilet block and showers, don't forget that finding one is only half the story. Once you get there, you need to decide where to best position yourself and then pitch properly to ensure the best night's sleep possible.

Location, location, location – Don't make the rookie mistake of pitching too close to the toilets and water facilities. It might seem handy at first, but bear in mind you'll probably be disturbed by other people making a visit there, both late into the night and early in the morning too. Equally, the furthest reaches of the site are best avoided, as this can be where those planning to stay up late, or to make a fair bit of noise, will position themselves. Try to opt for something in between.

Solid ground – You won't get a good night's sleep if you end up on uneven ground, so before you position the tent, lie down on the ground first to check it's a comfortable spot free of hidden holes, lumps and bumps or big rocks. You will rarely get a completely flat piece of ground to pitch on, but remember that on a slope – even a slight one – you need to keep your head uphill and your feet downhill, especially if there's more than one of you. You don't want to find yourselves sliding out of bed sideways and ending up in a heap at one end of the tent!

Check the wind direction – High winds can not only make your tent fabric flap and keep you up at night, but can also loosen guy lines too, with the result that you have to keep getting out and readjusting them throughout your stay. Position your tent so that the sharpest bit (perhaps a pole that juts out) faces the wind, to break it. If at all possible, keep your tent entrance away from the prevailing wind. Also, when pegging out your tent, position the guy lines into the wind and try to get a 90-degree angle between the lines and the pegs.

Wild camping?

If it's your first time to this particular area, no need to worry. Grab an Ordnance Survey map (either 1:25,000 or 1:50,000) and then you can pick out a great pitch before you even lay eyes on it in the flesh.

Look for somewhere away from towns and houses – you want to make sure you're staying well away from people's gardens. Lots of green on the map is a good sign.

You'll need a good water source nearby – look for river, which is shown by blue lines, or small or larger lakes, lochs or tarns, shown as patches of blue.

Now you need a way in – look for broken lines that indicate footpaths or bridleways. You'll need to pitch at least 50 m from them, but they are useful for getting you into the wilder spaces – especially at night.

Check out the contours – these are the lines marked with numbers that indicate the height of the land you'll be walking on. The closer together and more tightly clustered these are, the steeper the ground rises. The further apart, the more gentle the slope. You want as flat a ground as possible, so wide gaps in the contours are what you're looking for.

Know your symbols – watch out for green eyelash-like lines, which indicate soggy and boggy ground, not good for pitching a tent on, and usually a breeding ground for midges, so best avoided. Also look out for black circular-like shapes – indicating boulder fields. Again, not good for a sleeping mat!

You can always check out your chosen spot on Google Earth before you go, or check out photographs of the general area. The important thing is to have a couple of back-up spots prepared in case your first choice turns out to be unsuitable, or there's someone else already there!

Pitching problems

Whether on a campsite or in the wild, once you've picked your spot, pitching a tent should be a relatively straightforward affair – but what happens if you encounter a site with tricky ground? Fear not – there are some ways around it:

Problem: Hard or saturated ground
Solved: Rocks are your friends. If the ground is too tough to drive in a peg you can either use them as a makeshift hammer (be careful) or wrap the guy-lines around the rock and roll it up tight. Then place it on the ground, with two rocks in front of it to anchor it. On very wet ground a similar technique will work – as long as you have enough rocks to hold the cord in place.

Problem: You've lost your tent pegs
Solved: Look for branches with protruding sticks, as these will be easy to use as makeshift pegs. Use stronger wood as it will keep things in place better.

Problem: High wind
Solved: Use yourself and your kit! As soon as you've pitched, put your rucksack inside to act as a weight. Then, once inside, distribute your heaviest kit to each of the corners to act as extra ballast. If you don't have enough kit for this, use stones. Do remember that once you are safely inside, you yourself will be the best weight to keep your tent in place.

Problem: Guy lines are too short
Solved: See what you have to hand and improvise. Your rucksack will have a cord as will your sleeping bag 'stuff sack'.

Putting up your tent

Remember: Putting up a tent can be tricky – especially when the wind is blowing, the rain is lashing down and the kids are screaming. So, before you go on your camping trip, try putting up your tent at least once in your garden, so that it is more familiar (and also to check you have all the bits you need!). Much better to struggle with something when there's no audience or pressure.

Colourful clues – Poles are often colour-coded so you know which sleeves they fit through and which holes they go into. This can save time when you're pitching in the elements. If the poles don't come this way, then it's worth colour-coding them before you go to avoid wrestling with instructions once you're there.

Don't panic – Struggling with your tent is all part of being a camper – it happens to the best of us. Take a deep breath, look at the instructions and try again – arguing with each other has never resulted in erecting a tent any faster!

Packing tricks

The more you camp, the more you become familiar with the kit you have to use and, in doing so, you learn how to best use it and re-pack it. Here are some hard-won packing tips...

Getting your sleeping bag back in its sack

Often this is achieved after a prolonged period of shouting and swearing! However there *is* a trick to it. If you have a down bag, then simply stuff it into the sack; if it's synthetic then rolling will usually be easier. Buy yourself a compression sack and, once the bag is inside, pull the draw-cords to close it, sit on it to remove the extra air, and you can then tighten the compression straps, getting your bag to its smallest size.

Top tip

Once back home, remember to take your bag out of the stuff sack, or compression sack, and store it in a larger bag so that the insulation doesn't stay compacted. If compacted, it won't work as well at keeping you warm next time you need it.

How to pack up a tent in the rain

There's no sugar-coating this – you *will* get wet. The key is to do everything you can, inside and out, before you remove the outer sheet. If possible, unclip the inner sheet first and pack this away inside the tent so that it remains dry. Before you take the structure down (providing it's not very windy) remove the tent pegs first. That way, when you're ready, you can take the outer sheet off in one go. Be sure to shake the fabric well before packing it away in its bag, in order to remove large puddles of water that may have gathered.

Top tip

Don't be lazy! As soon as you get home, unpack the wet tent and dry it thoroughly for a couple of days. Don't pack it away again until it has completely dried out.

Pack your tent in a rucksack

Don't be confined by the bag that your tent came in. The most effective way of packing a tent in a rucksack is to split up the parts. So, remove the poles and stow them on the side of your rucksack. Put the tent pegs in the top of your bag or a front pocket. And, if there's more than one of you, split the inner and outer sheets between you to share the weight and bulk.

Top tip

Buy a dry bag for the tent fabric – that way you can stuff it down as small as possible so that it takes up less room.

Packing your camping gear for travel

If you're flying, you obviously won't be able to take your pegs and (possibly) poles as hand luggage, as security rules are very tight. But you *can* take the fabric if you need to – so at least if something did go missing, you could improvise. Some countries are very strict about bringing in outdoor gear, due to contaminants that may be on them from soil, for example. So do make sure your kit is clean before you pack it. Consider taking a groundsheet or 'tarp' to deal with difficult terrain. Remember that camping gas can never be taken on a plane.

Top tip

Do a little bit of research before you go in order to find out where the nearest camping shop is to where you will be staying – that way you can replace anything you need to and also stock up on supplies without wasting time once you've arrived.

CHAPTER 5

CAMPING CAPERS

'Most campsites are like suburbs, with neatly defined pitches… and fellow campers who are over-concerned with the condition of the toilet.'

MATTHEW DE ABAITUA, *THE ART OF CAMPING*

No matter whether you know it or not, there are nine types of camper out there – and you, my friend, are one of them. Would you rather stay at campsites or in the mountains? Blow all your cash on kit or get right back to basics? It's time to find out what kind of camper you are…

1. The Mild Camper

Happiest when on a proper campsites with flushing loos, you've been doing this long enough to come prepared with everything you need to be comfortable – but not flashy. You arrive to a campsite in plenty of time to find a good pitch – close enough to the bathrooms to be convenient, but far enough away to escape the smells. Enjoying the simple tasks like cooking with limited equipment, you still like to know you've got neighbours close by to ask for any bits of kit you've forgotten or to share a marshmallow with come the evening. You like to have a hot shower on tap, too. Sure, the occupants of the tent next door may keep you awake with their snoring; the neighbours on the other side wake you up just a little too early than you'd like, and you may sometimes wish that the couple with the kids across the way would go to bed a little earlier, but then you remember that this is a community. It is a way for you to escape on a budget break with the family. It might not be perfect, but it's where you'd always rather be.

2. The Cool Camper

Did you know you can buy a tent that is an exact to-scale replica of a VW camper van? If the answer is 'no', then I am sad to say that you clearly don't fit into this category; if the answer is, 'yes – but did you know you can also order your personalised number plate to go with it?', then it's safe to assume that this is you! You are the one whose pitch oozes campsite cool – whether the proud owner of a tent that looks like something else (camper van, London Underground carriage, a slice of watermelon), or the person pioneering inflatable tent poles – because metal ones were so 'last year' – you make the rest of us in a simple tunnel tent green with envy. It doesn't matter that your fancy model weights twice as much as ours – and is twice as draughty. It matters not that your inflatable poles are a nightmare to deflate come the end of the weekend, it is you who make the site entertaining and camping seriously cool… and *don't* you know it?!

3. The Glamper

One stage further from the cool camper is the luxury-loving rough-it-but-don't-make-me-feel-like-I'm-really-camping 'glamper'. No doubt sporting Hunter wellies and denim shorts, and with hair so shiny and straight you look like you've just stepped out of a salon, you are all about getting back to nature as though you were still at home. Forget designer tents (though you probably have one in your cupboard at home made by Ted Baker or Cath Kidston), for you it's all about the yurt, bell tent or safari-style canvas lodge, complete with proper chairs, beds with mattresses and duvets – definitely not sleeping bags, thank you very much! It's not that you're not into the great outdoors; it's just that you don't think there's any reason to do it without creature comforts. So bring on the wine coolers, crank up the tent heaters, unpack the solar-powered coffee maker – and if all that comes with a price tag of £300+ for a weekend, then so be it. Champagne anyone?

4. The Gear Nut

Bio-fuel camping stove that also charges your stereo – check! Limited edition Victorinox expedition Swiss army knife – check! That thing you plug in to your iPhone to make it a satellite phone – check! If this sounds like your typical packing list before a camping trip then, know it or not, you are a gear nut. Boasting all the latest techno advances manufacturers can throw at you, you are like a walking gear catalogue – which of course would be a digital version held on a watch that could project images onto the walls of your tent, while also getting your email and editing your latest homemade adventure movie at the same time. From portable pressure showers to 'smart' head torches, thanks to your kit bag, you're always prepared for any eventuality, be it food shortage, extreme Arctic conditions or zombie apocalypse – and who cares that you're only on a campsite in Surrey? When things get serious, you know you can survive – if only you knew where you put your phone charger…

5. The Wild Camper

Who needs a shower block? This could easily be your mantra. Where others crave their creature comforts, you can get by without, and so head out, with the lightest kit you can get, into the crowd-free places: in the middle of the mountains, by wild lakes, on secluded beaches. Sure, it will mean digging your own toilet, and, true, you may get a little cold, but the chance to pick your own pitch and to wake up in a truly rugged place, with the grass as your mattress and the mountain as your headboard, is what made you leave the campsites in the first place. Never mind the battery-powered fairy lights; you sleep with a string of stars above you. Forget the mod cons, the snoring neighbours and the campsite politics, you'll choose the extra effort required to walk with all your kit on your back if it means you get to watch the sun rise from a mountaintop while everyone else is still in bed. And better yet… it costs nothing at all.

6. The Survivalist

Wild campers – pah! Carrying in a dehydrated meal and a proper sleeping mat is practically 'glamping' as far as you're concerned. No, *you* want to live off the land – and I mean *really* live off it – from your khaki backpack that hides your mushroom identification guide, to the bushcraft knife you never leave home without. Complete with your trusty fire-steel for building and making your very own cooker later, you like to strip everything back down to basics. You prefer to 'bivvy' or better yet 'tarp', rather than 'tent' it and, when it comes to first aid, you know you can always find some sphagnum moss to disinfect any wounds. Self-sufficient and resourceful, you can craft a spoon, bowl and even sleeping mat from a set of reeds, and navigate your way back to civilisation using the North Star and the decomposing body of a stoat. Your ideal camping companion would be Bear Grylls or Ray Mears – because you know you could certainly teach *them* a thing or two!

7. The Organiser

Probably a former scout or Duke of Edinburgh Award leader, you know that everything will be alright as long as we all keep a tidy camp. You'll have packed your kit at least a week before your trip with meticulous detail, and brought extra supplies of the basics with you in case someone else has forgotten theirs and you need to help them out. You'll have a well-practised procedure for pitching your tent quickly and efficiently – which you will have naturally fine-tuned in the months before this by trying it out in your back garden first. When your tent neighbour rolls up, you'll think nothing of instructing them on where they should place their tent pegs and sharing all the tips you've garnered over the years about the only correct way to secure the flysheet. Your cooking happens with military precision and you are the on-site 'go-to' person if there's a problem because you can initiate the proper complaints procedure. Perhaps not the most carefree, you are the most appreciated person on any campsite where you may find yourself.

8. The Partying Camper

Boasting a tent with blackened walls (so you can sleep well past lunchtime) and a huge flag designating your pitch (so you can easily identify it later after a few too many), you view heading into the outdoors, far away from the confines of four brick walls, as the perfect excuse to celebrate. Fresh air, open spaces, the ability to share your love for music and open fires in the same setting, the night-time is when you come alive. Sure, those guys in the neighbouring tent looked a little apprehensive when you first arrived and started snapping your glow-sticks, but just wait till you start playing your best guitar jam. You have *great* musical taste that you just can't wait to share with all these lucky strangers, and you are going to tell them what a great time you are having by whooping and hollering your appreciation way past midnight. Party on!

9. The Reluctant Camper

We know that you haven't actually bought this book for *you* – you're just flicking through its pages deciding whether or not to get it for your camping mad partner/friend/parent. Yes, that same camping-mad person who drags you off to Pwllheli year on year, tent in tow, whether you like it or not. You'd think by now you'd be used to it, had come to terms with the wet tent walls in the morning, the necessity to put on shoes, socks and coats just to get up in the night for a quick wee, and the inability to ever have a private conversation that your neighbours can't hear, and yet every time you reluctantly head off camping again you do so with a heavy heart. But at least you don't complain about it. Much.

Campsite Capers

Camping is great fun, but what else can you do to make your camping trips entertaining? Here are a few ideas…

In-tent entertainment

I-Spy: An oldie but a goodie, camping I-spy is more challenging as there's only so many objects you can see and make people guess at – then you have to get really inventive: D for damp patch, for instance, or I for inflatable dog bowl…

Happy campers: Make sure you have some sheets of paper and pens. Then give them out to each camper. Fold the paper into three. Everyone draws the head of a typical happy camper on the first third of paper. Then they fold the paper over so no one can see what they've drawn. Everyone passes their paper on and then draws a torso, folding that over and passing the paper on. Finally, everyone draws the legs. When it's all done, reveal the happy camper you've drawn – weird and wonderful results guaranteed!

Once upon a campsite: This is a storytelling game. Appoint one member of the group as story editor. They choose the theme of the story. The first person then tells the first three sentences of a story starting with 'Once upon a campsite'. The editor then selects the next person to introduce the first character, and that person adds three sentences. Then the editor selects the next person to add another character/an event/a twist and so on, until the story is done. The best part is it can be as short or as long as you want!

What am I?: Simple but fun. One person thinks of an object/animal and then each member of the group is allowed three questions to work out what it is.

Spot the difference: Gather together as much of your smaller camping gear as you can and place it in the centre of the tent. Once done, the group can spend 10 seconds looking at it then they have to turn around. Remove one item and the group turns back and must then try to work out what's missing.

Out-of-canvas capers

First one to find: A scavenger hunt, this is a great one to play with kids. Set them a challenge to find a number of items such as a stone shaped like a heart, a yellow leaf, a worm, etc., and then get them to bring their finds back to camp to show the group. It's a good idea to have treats as rewards too!

Night-time walk: Once the sun goes down, consider heading into the dark for a wander. You don't have to go too far to appreciate how different things look at night. Notice how a sheep's eyes glow in the beam of a head torch, how much further away things can seem in the darkness, or how bright things can actually be when lit by the moon. Then turn your light off and listen. You'll be amazed as you notice a *plethora* of sounds – from owls calling to bats swooping – and even leaves falling off the trees.

Obstacle course: Obviously do be careful that you don't annoy fellow campers with this idea, but campsites really are great places for physical games. Set up a course with branches and leaves – in the sand if near a beach, amongst trees if by a forest – and time each other as to who can complete it fastest. A very good way to warm up on a cold day, too!

Cloud watching: Watching the stars twinkling is fantastic, but you don't have to wait till night falls to gaze up at the sky. Head outside during the day and then spot all the different shapes of the clouds or try to identify the different types – cirrus, cumulonimbus, stratus – they will all help you gauge the state of the weather too!

CHAPTER 6

AROUND THE WORLD

*'When you have to wait a year to sleep next
to a tree, something is wrong.'*

GEORGE CARLIN

Camping Fact

14.9 %

In 2011, **42.5 million** Americans went camping
(14.9 per cent of the country)
– up by 2.6 million from 2010.

They spent an average of 12.6 days
camping per person per year.

(2012 American Camper Report)

If you think that it's all about tents you erect in fields then think again, because the world offers a vast array of camping options for the intrepid. On the following pages are a few that should go on your wish-list…

Some of the more far-flung places Brits camp outside of Europe:

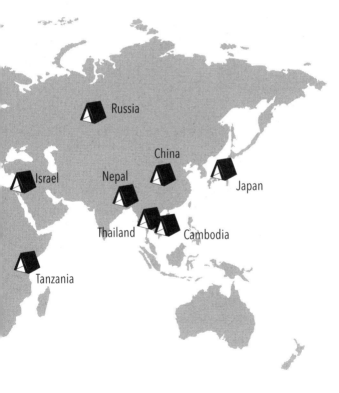

Russia

China

Israel

Nepal

Japan

Thailand

Cambodia

Tanzania

(Go Outdoors Camping Survey, 2014)

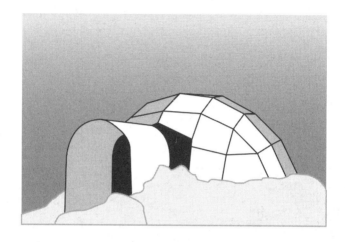

1. Aurora Pods, Finland

Forget emergency snow-holes or winter 'bivvies', a hotel in Finland has turned the idea of 'igloo camping' on its head. Constructed from thermal glass and protruding from the snow like giant mirror-balls, these glass igloos are not only heated and feature a proper bed, but they also allow you uninterrupted views of the crystal clear night sky. And, as the aurora borealis (the Northern Lights) appear above this town on an average of 200 nights each year, the odds are definitely in your favour.

More info: www.kakslauttanen.fi/

2. Everest South Base Camp, Nepal

If you're going to stick with a tent, then you may as well head to, arguably, the most famous campsite in the world. Not a site in the traditional sense as there are no designated pitches and, as far as facilities are concerned, it's a case of bringing your own Sherpas to carry the Portaloo, in terms of historical significance it's still got to feature on the 'to do' list of every serious camper. Pitch here and you'll sleep on the surface of the Khumbu Glacier, listening to it rumble and squeak deep below your sleeping mat. From your tent flap at 5,364 m you'll see some epic mountain views as well as the infamous icefall that leads up the side of the highest mountain in the world. To camp here you will need to be part of a pre-arranged group organised through a tour operator and you will - of course - pay for the privilege; but to be able to linger in the very place from where mountaineering adventures began, is a priceless experience.

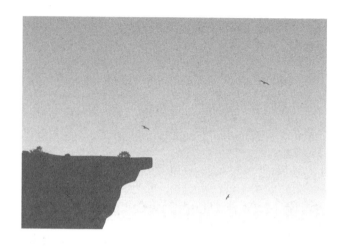

3. Mountain ledges, Jordan

Everyone heading to this part of the Arabian Peninsula will undoubtedly go to Petra; the iconic Rose Red city sees the bulk of visitors. But camping fans should head to Wadi Rum. Also known as the Valley of the Moon, you can hire your own Bedouin guide and hike amongst the wind-scoured sandstone rock. Come sundown, you can of course sleep in a tent if you want to, but the more adventurous do like the Bedouins and simply sleep out on blankets on a rocky ledge, watching the stars overhead while listening to the crackle from the campfire.

4. Sleep in a swag, Australia

Like a 'bivvy bag', but more luxurious, the Australian swag bag is a rolled up mattress and sheet that you pop your sleeping bag into, often with a built-in bug shield. It may not sound much to protect you from all the insects and poisonous snakes that linger in the Outback but, believe me, once you've watched the light play on Uluru at sunset and are curled up in your 'swag' watching the night sky twinkle overhead, those critters will be the last thing on your mind.

5. Hanging tents, Germany

If you go down to the woods at Waldseilgarten, you'll soon have a camping surprise. There, among the trees, are a dozen hanging tents suspended from the branches at various heights. Featuring a fabric-covered platform supported by a metal frame, they are suspended from a secured single point. Getting in to the accommodation will require some basic rope training – as will getting out to go to the toilet – but being surrounded by the stunning Bavarian mountain and forest scenery at Pronten will make all the effort worthwhile… just maybe go easy on the alcohol before you go to bed!

More info: www.waldseilgarten-hoellschlucht.de/

6. Teepees, Washington, USA

A mainstay of 'glamping', it's not hard these days to find somewhere in the world to experience the delights of snuggling down in your spacious, pyramidal abode. Formed from a series of poles secured together at the top and covered in canvas or – more traditionally – animal hide, they once provided shelter to Native Americans in the plains and prairies of North America. The best place to experience this is, of course, the USA. Head to Yakima in Washington State and you can first learn about these self-sufficient and resourceful people on the reserve at nearby Toppenish before heading to Zillah. Here, a woman called Pepper rents out 22 ft teepees with luxurious beds, private toilets and an open air bathhouse and shower room too – with all money received going to help her rescue horses. The ultimate camping experience with a feel-good vibe.

More info: www.cherrywoodbbandb.com

7. Cliff camping, Colorado, USA

Once only the realm of the Big Wall Climbers – who pitch up in porta-ledges (basic tents suspended on the side of cliffs through a series of ropes) – now a number of mountaineers are realising that more and more tent aficionados are keen to experience the thrill of a high altitude sleep. One such place is Rocky Mountain National Park, where you can sign up for a bedroom aside a vertical rock face, learn how to 'rappel ascend' a rope to get you in and out of your shelter and even make breakfast on your little ledge after a night spent where the eagles soar.

More info: www.kmaconline.com/cliff-camping-colorado

8. Hobbit hole, Wales

Fans of Tolkien's work will know all too well what to expect when hearing this moniker. Though not quite as lush as the abodes in Hobbiton itself, this Welsh hideaway, in Abersoch, is a rounded and insulated camping pod. With proper beds, plug sockets, a small heater, a lockable door and even a TV aerial point, it's more on the glamour side of camping than anything else; but if it gets you into the outdoors and offers the chance to explore this coastal corner of Wales, then embrace this elaborate 'tent' with all the gusto of Bilbo Baggins!

More info: www.the-willows-abersoch.co.uk

9. Tented camp, Kenya

Whisk yourself over to Africa to watch the annual Masai Mara Great Migration – where wildebeest make the treacherous journey through the bush between July and October. As for sleeping arrangements, you can forget a regular tent! Amid the rolling grasslands, acacia woods and distant mountains, you'll bed down at your chosen tented camp – think four-poster wooden beds, hardwood floors, all draped in fabric. Sometimes raised up like tree-houses, and often constructed around a central dining tent, these camps are always steeped in old world charm. For a true night in the wild, this wonderful accommodation simply can't be beaten.

10. Maharaja tent, India

India. The very word conjures up the smell of spices, the sounds of an infinite chaos and the collaboration of bold colour on sari fabrics. A visit will always leave you wanting more, but sleeping in a lavish Maharaja tent will have you finding even more excuses not to leave. There's ample opportunity for camping in this vast country, but for a pitch with historical flavour, head to the small town of Maheshwar, and the Alhilya Fort. This eighteenth-century building looms above a meandering river, where *ghats* (steps) take you up to its courtyard and turrets. The rooms are lovely, but the special Maharaja tent, pitched on the riverbank, is superb and offers its own plunge pool and fine dining.

More info: www.ahilyafort.com

11. Sleep in the Empty Quarter, Oman

Oman may be known for its gold-covered opulence, but that doesn't mean there's no place for tents. With choices abounding from the rolling desert of Wahiba Sands or the mystically named Empty Quarter – made famous by explorer Wilfred Thesiger in 1946 – you can go hiking by day, then camp by night, away from the glitz and glamour of Muscat. If you want to add a touch of Omani luxury to the experience, then organise something with one of the hotels, who will send you into the wilderness accompanied by staff who construct sumptuous tents for you. The tents come complete with private toilet and shower, cotton sheets and toiletries and, before you relax in your carpeted bed chamber, you are served freshly cooked meals from local produce. Blimey!

12. Whitepods, Switzerland

Half tent, half mountain hut, these Swiss structures dot the slopes in the Alps, offering jaw-dropping views from their bay windows. Taking the tent-like geodesic structure as its muse, these shelters are constructed as a network of triangles, to give them strength against the snow that surrounds them come winter. They even offer a terrace, marrying the best of the outdoor camping experience with the warmth and convenience of an Alpine hut.

More info: www.whitepod.com

13. Camp among wild wolves, Michigan, USA

While Yellowstone National Park may be famous for successfully reintroducing wolves, there is actually a better spot to camp out and experience these creatures in the USA - Isle Royale. Officially the least visited National Park in the USA, it gets fewer visitors each year than Great Smoky Mountains National Park gets in a single day. Seemingly floating in Lake Superior, it is 72 km in length and 14 km wide, has no roads but does boast several campsites. Some have facilities, and many can only be accessed by the water. Isle Royale is populated by moose that first swam across from the mainland over a hundred years ago, later joined by their natural predators - wolves. Now, both make for a unique wildlife-watching experience. And, as the sun sets, you can snuggle in your tent and listen to these primeval canines howling at the moon.

More info: www.nps.gov

14. Find peace in Hiroshima, Japan

Mention Hiroshima, and one thing comes to mind: the poignant historic event, when this small, unassuming city was devastated by the dropping of the A-Bomb in 1945. It may be somewhat surprising, therefore, to realise that it is home to one of the most peaceful places in Japan. Sitting in the city's bay is Miyajima Island (or Itsukushima as it is officially known, but seldom called). The name means 'the Shrine Island'. Covered with a mass of sacred sites – from Buddhist temples to a floating *torii* gate that is reached by boat at high tide, then walkable when the tide goes out – it a place that offers both outer and inner peace. Amid the wild fallow deer you can pitch you tent in a forest of camphor and cypress trees – and bookings aren't even required in advance.

More info: www.visit-miyajima-japan.com

15. EcoCamp, Patagonia

OK, so getting here might not be the best way to boost your green credentials – given the long-haul flight required for many of us – but once you've reached this Chilean outpost, nestled in the middle of the Torres del Paine National Park, you can 'camp' in eco-style in a tent-like geodesic dome. Looking distinctly yurt-like, but with a twist, you can gaze up at the Patagonian landscape from your window knowing that sustainable materials have built your abode and that the no-electricity policy makes this eco-experience as sustainable as regular camping – though in a little more comfort. Better yet, hiking trails abound from your doorstep. Happy camping!
www.ecocamp.travel

Camping Fact

About three million people camp at parks run by the US National Park Service every year, according to the Outdoor Industry Association.

Camping Fact

In 2013, the University of Colorado did a study into the effects of artificial light on the human body clock. They monitored a group that were exposed to a normal (small) dose of outdoor light and indoor lighting each day for a week and then made them camp for a week with natural light only (no electric lights allowed). They found that people whose body clock is synchronised with sunrise and sunset – as campers are – experienced better physical and mental health than those who don't. So that's why camping makes us happy – even when it rains…

Best of British

Despite the lure of overseas, the UK is still popular among Brits as a camping destination, with 65 per cent choosing it over an overseas tent-bound adventure. But where in the UK is the most popular? Turn over to find out...

Top ten UK camping destinations

Scottish Highlands

Isle of Skye,
Scotland

Lake District

Yorkshire

Derbyshire

Snowdonia

Shell Island
(North Wales)

Devon

New Forest

Cornwall

(Go Outdoors Camping Survey, 2014)

As fun as it is to travel the world, Britain is also a fantastic place to pitch a tent. It's easy to get around, and offers myriad landscapes within an easy distance – from coast to moor, mountain to forest. For an ultimate slice of the UK under canvas, try one of these campsites…

Long Beach campsite, Scotland

www.knoydart-foundation.com

Up in the northwest reaches of Scotland, a peninsula stretches out to sea. Sandwiched between two lochs – Loch Nevis and Loch Hourn (also known as the lochs of heaven and hell) – is the land known as Knoydart – oft cited as the 'Last Great Wilderness'. On it there is only one stretch of road – a 7 km strip of tarmac that runs from the harbour to the cluster of houses at Inverie. It is the only road that is not connected to the rest of Britain's mainland network. Access here is only by ferry or a very long walk. The chief claim to fame here is the Old Forge (Britain's most remote pub). But, for us tent lovers, it is the campsite on Long Beach that has the celebrity status. There are minimal facilities (you may be able to use the bunkhouse showers if you're lucky), but its location cannot be beaten. Sitting at the head of the water, with views out to the isles of Skye, Rum and Eigg, it offers panoramas that money just can't buy – but at only £4 a night, they are still instantly affordable!

Cleadale, Isle of Eigg, Scotland

www.eiggorganics.co.uk

For a proper island adventure you can't beat a trip to Eigg. Dominated by a giant pitchstone ridge that protrudes from the grass like a notch in an old tree trunk, its shape alone is iconic. The one and only campsite on the isle is on the west side and rewards those with tents with a perfect view of the Atlantic Ocean and the Outer Hebrides. It is also close to another geological phenomenon known as the singing sands – or *Traigh a' Bhigeil* – a quartzite beach which makes an audible squeak as you walk across it. Explore by day then bed down in your £5-a-night bargain site by night, complete with flushing toilets and showers. An enchanting, atmospheric place.

Turner Hall Farm, Lake District

www.duddonvalley.co.uk

It can be difficult to find a quiet spot in the ever-popular Lakes – but not so at this campsite. Open from March to November it is a sprawling site of fields, boulders and trees and, if you pick the right spot, you can feel as if you're not really on a campsite at all. The place has a sense of somewhere wild, away from all mod cons. But, thankfully you're not! With on-site showers, toilets and a pub within a five to ten minute walk away, you get the perfect mix of mild and wild camping in one hit – and for only £6 per person.

Aberafon, Wales

www.aberafon.co.uk

Sixteen. That's the total number of pitches on this little Welsh campsite, perched on the edge of the Llyn Peninsula. Squeezed between the shapely three-pronged peak of Yr Eifl and hanging above the rough waves of the coast, if you pitch your tent here you feel like you're practically positioned on the sand. With a smattering of rock pools across the land outside your tent flap, and the sea on your very doorstep this, for the hardy, is the place where wild campsite meets wild swimming! And, for those who are even more adventurous, there's a paragliding school nearby. No matter which way you look at this place, from the air, sea or the inside of a tent, this site is one of the most enticing in Wales.

Treen Farm Campsite, Penzance

www.treenfarmcampsite.co.uk

Down in the southern reaches of mainland Britain, just shy by a few kilometres of Land's End, sits Treen Farm. An easy meander from some of the best patches of sand in this part of the country, and close by the surf-perfect coves, it's a heavenly place to pitch a tent. Not only does it offer cliff top views over the Cornish coast but it also sells local meat and vegetable produce from the onsite shop. They even stock organic pasteurised milk from their local cows – and all from just £5 a night. Bargain!

CHAPTER 7

EXTREME CAMPING
— THE NEXT LEVEL

*'The person with the fewest possessions is
the freest. Thoreau was right.'*
Paul Theroux, *The Happy Isles of Oceania*

Camping is simple. You take a tent into a designated field, pay some money, and then get to pitch up and make use of the toilet and shower facilities, right? Wrong! Since the hobby began, there have been a hardy few who have pushed the boundaries further and further, and now the term 'camping' can appear with a surprising number of prefixes in front of it. From 'extreme' to 'wild', if you've got a thirst for adventure and a need for an adrenaline rush, then why not experiment with your pitching…

Backyard camping

In 2011, a lady called Victoria Webbon started an online community called Campinmygarden.com. Her aim? To encourage people to look beyond the traditional campsite and, instead, venture no further than other people's backyards. Building a network of members from small terrace houses to the sprawling acres of country retreats, her idea was to enable private homeowners to open their free spaces up to visitors. With a number of options available from the so-called 'bamping' (basic camping) to 'glamping' (glamorous camping), some destinations are free and some command a small fee. Most have very basic facilities, i.e. a toilet only, but it's a great – and cheap – way to tour the world with your tent.

Wild camping

> *'Wild country [is] a means of reassuring ourselves of our sanity as creatures, a part of the geography of hope.'*
> WALLACE STEGNER

Increasingly popular as regular camping becomes more and more mainstream, 'wild camping' is simply that – heading off into the wilds, be it forest, mountains, beach or cave – and pitching your tent there. No people, no campsite politics and (as long as you do it right) no problems.

Am I allowed to do it?

Among mountaineers, hill-walkers and climbers it really isn't a new concept. Sleeping in the hills has been done since at least the last century, and even beyond, making it more socially acceptable than officially legal. In Scotland, thanks to the Land Reform Act 2003, wild camping is perfectly legal (with the exception of the shores of Loch Lomond). This is also the case in Dartmoor, where the right to wild camping falls under the National Parks and Access to the Countryside Act 1949. And, in 2014, the Welsh Government began discussions to see if they too could legalise the activity in their National Parks. Elsewhere, you're supposed to ask the landowner's permission before sleeping on their land, but this is often difficult to ascertain and tricky to do in practice. If you do 'wild camp' you will usually be fine, provided you remain discreet and follow the basic unwritten wild camping rules...

1. Arrive late and leave early – You shouldn't just pitch up in the middle of the day. Plan to be there as it's starting to get dark and be packed up and away by the time other walkers are around.

2. Never light an open fire – The places you are likely to be heading to have a high risk of fire; you don't want to be responsible for destroying acres of beautiful landscape! Worried about being cold? Take more layers with you.

3. Leave no trace – Make sure you carry out your rubbish; as the proverb goes – take only pictures, leave only footsteps.

4. Be considerate – Respect the privacy of others; if asked to move on by the landowner, do so without argument. Remember, if you're polite, you'll more likely to be allowed to stay.

5. Camp high – Stay well away from people's houses, pathways and cattle fields, keep it discreet and you should have no problems.

6. Poo responsibly – Find a sheltered spot at least 50 m away from water and downstream of popular camping areas. Dig a 15-20 cm deep hole, and replace the earth once you have finished your business. Carry your toilet roll, and any sanitary products, out with your other rubbish.

Where shall I do it?

If it's your first time, go somewhere you know wild camping is legally allowed. Then the only worry is whether or not you remembered to bring the camping gas! Look for somewhere that is well away from houses and roads, somewhere offering flat ground, near a water source (e.g. river or lake) and not too exposed – so don't climb to the top of a mountain for your first trip! Geographically, if in the UK, there are two places you should consider, as they both allow wild camping:

Dartmoor

In the wilds of south Devon, this vast and tor-dotted moorland offers endless possibilities for wild camping. Thanks to its geographical location in England's sunnier southwest, the weather tends to be better than the more mountainous places further north, and you can camp in most locations within the park worry-free. Remember that the weather can change quickly, so always pack waterproofs and extra warm layers – and get an Ordnance Survey map before you go. Some of the area lies within military training zones, so you'll need to check in advance for localised closures. For tips on where to camp, any seasonal restrictions and army firing times, check out www.dartmoor.npa.gov.uk.

Scotland

You really are spoilt for choice once you are north of the border. You might decide on the lower Southern Uplands – great for stargazing as it is an official Dark Sky Reserve (the Northern Lights have even been spotted here); the moors and mountains around Glen Coe – home to the quivering quagmire that is Rannoch Moor as well as the iconic Lost Valley and the Three Sisters (mountain peaks); or the many majestic mountain peaks and passes around Ben Nevis – the highest mountain in the UK. The often snow-covered mountains of the easternmost Cairngorms are home to the only wild reindeer herd in Britain. Or you could choose a beach like Sandwood Bay in the far north – over a mile long! The only way to access it is by walking for 2–3 hours. They really do call this marvellous country 'bonny Scotland' for a good reason!

Beyond the tent

Going wild may mean that you need to invest in something different from a standard tent. As you're trying to leave as little impact as possible you need something small, lightweight and easy to pitch and remove quickly. Turn over for four suggestions for wild campers...

1. Bivvy bags

Only big enough for you, your sleeping mat and sleeping bag (everything else needs to stay outside so take waterproof bags too), in their basic form they offer a waterproof sack, and at the high end, a hooped head section with a built-in bug shield and waterproof cover, plus extra venting to help with moisture. They pack down into the size of a beer can, and can tuck into some tiny ledges and cracks in the landscape to really make you feel a part of it. The main downside is that, no matter the weather, you will get wet, as condensation from your body heat will always build up. So, using a synthetic sleeping bag rather than down – is highly recommended.

Best used: On summer nights when there's little chance of rain, so you can lie back and watch the sun slip down into night and see the stars come out to dance above.

2. Tarps

A simple sheet of waterproof fabric that you can stretch out between trees, stones or walking poles, a tarp is a great weight-friendly option, especially when camping somewhere warm. They can protect you from a rain shower but, equally, will shade you from the burning sunshine. If using a tarp by itself you will certainly get close to nature, as there are no fabric walls around you. It's recommended that you still take a groundsheet, or at least a camping mat, to stay warm and dry. And, if you can afford to, get a waterproof sleeping bag.

Best used: In warm and humid conditions or if 'bivving' in the rain – a tarp and bivvy bag make an ideal combination in wetter conditions.

3. Hammock

For a wild night in the forest or high on a tree-topped peak, you can't beat the hammock for its ability to lull you to sleep swinging gently in the breeze. Of course you are limited to terrain where there are suitable anchor points to attach it to, and if it looks like rain, or you're surrounded by biting insects, you will also need a tarp and mosquito net, respectively. Some bags come with both of those built in. Light and quirky, every serious camper has *got* to try one at least once.
Best used: In the forest in summertime, to be gently rocked into a truly wild slumber.

4. Roof-top tent

Originally invented for safaris – people don't enjoy the idea of potentially being woken up by a curious lion while bedding down on the ground. They range from small two-man jobs that attach to pick-ups, camper vans and Land Rovers, (courtesy of a built-in roof rack and retractable ladder), to four-bedroom numbers with space for kayaks. They're certainly not the kind of shelter you look for to go discreetly into the mountains, but for a pre-walk night out in style they are a great idea to spice up the start and finish of an on-foot adventure.
Best used: On an overlanding trip where you will be returning to your car at night.

Extreme camping

Think that wild camping is too tame? Why not step it up with one of these options…

Portaledge: Head to a big wall climbing hotspot, such as Yosemite in California, and you'll often see a series of tents dangling from sheer vertical cliffs. Called 'portaledges', these temporary tent structures are erected by climbers and secured onto the rock with well-positioned bolts and a series of carabiners and ropes. The tents themselves are fairly basic, single skin affairs, but when there's nothing but a small suspended platform between you and hundreds of metres of air, condensation is really the least of your worries!

Snow-holes: Used in extreme places like the Arctic in an emergency, or even in Scotland for training in winter skills, a snow-hole can either help protect you from the elements (ensuring you warm up just in the act of making one) or help you survive a life-or-death scenario. Literally a hole dug into snow, you can go on courses to learn this survival technique. It's not recommended that you do this without receiving expert training, however.

Caves: Not necessarily underground, these naturally formed crevices can appear on the side of a mountain, at the bottom of a hill or are even formed by a sliding boulder perched on top of many other stones. Normally damp and often draughty, they may not be most people's idea of a good night out, but to the 'extreme sleeper' they represent some proper excitement away from the norm. If you want to try it, make sure that you check out the cave first to make sure it's safe and doesn't present a flood risk. And it's also recommended that you take a bivvy bag as it will be wet!

Extreme Sleeps

No, not hanging off cliff faces – these are places to pitch at the extremes of the compass…

Northernmost campsite in the world

Far in the reaches of the Arctic, in the Svalbard Archipelago, is the island of Spitsbergen. Up towards the west of the most northern settlement of Longyearbyen is the world's northernmost public campsite. Here you can stumble from your tent in the morning to see terns nesting and the sun rising on the edge of the lagoon that sits at your tent flap. Of course there are wild options further north, but then you will have to take a polar bear alarm with you…

Southernmost campsite in the world

Though not officially given the accolade (there are many wild/free camping spots that may fight for the title) certainly one of the most southern-sited official campsites lies in the world's southernmost city of Ushuaia, in Argentina. Called La Pista Del Andino, it's just up the road from the Beagle Channel which is the gateway to Antarctica. It's from this place that many an expedition cruise sets off, and icebergs can often be spotted in the area.

Highest campsite in the world

Situated on the lower slopes of Mount Everest is the highest campsite in the world. Located at 5,364 m above sea level, it sits on the southern (Nepalese) side of the world's highest mountain. Less visited (by trekkers) is the one on the northern (Tibetan) side at 5,150 m. Though you won't find tents there year-round, the spot is permanently marked with colourful prayer flags.

Lowest campsite in the world

At 427 m below sea level, bordered by both Israel and Jordan, is the lowest point on earth – the Dead Sea. And, if you fancy it, you can camp right next to it. The Ein Gedi Beach Campground in Jordan offers tent-lovers the chance to sleep right beside its saline waters so you can nip out for that dip whenever you want. Located on the northern shore, you're as close to the lowest point as you can get.

> ### *Did you know?*
>
> *You can actually go camping in Antarctica now. A number of expedition cruises offer 'regular' people the chance to spend a night on ice on the Antarctic Peninsula, or on one of the islands around it; with no training, raised sponsorship money or hard work required! Where do we sign up?*

Record-breaking campers

We campers are an ambitious lot – and we've quite a number of World Records to our names. Check them out…

Longest marshmallow roasting stick

Held by American camping fan Gregg Spiridellis – he managed to roast his 'mallows' on a 129.50-inch stick in June 2014, beating the previous records of 78 and 96 inches set in 2009 and 2011, respectively.

Largest group of campers doing 'The Wave'

A total of 300 tent-dwellers set a record, in August 2012, for the most campers doing a wave. Students at the ID Tech Camp at Stamford University are the current record holders.

Most campers wearing paper crowns

It was a proud day for the UK Camping and Caravanning Club in 2012. They decided to mark the Queen's Diamond Jubilee by setting a new world record for the most number of people wearing paper crowns for a 24-hour period. A total of 14,621 campers took part in over 100 sites across the UK, claiming the prize.

In 2007, Andy Strangeway became the first person to camp on all 162 of Scotland's islands.

And, in 2014, the author of this book, Phoebe Smith, became the first woman to camp at all the extreme points of mainland Britain on consecutive nights – these included the highest, lowest, northernmost, southernmost, easternmost and westernmost points of the country. She was the first person to include the centre of Britain in her quest.

BUSHCRAFT BASICS

'Bushcraft is what you carry in your mind and your muscles.'
RAY MEARS

Advances in camping technology are fantastic – we can make French press coffee by the camping stove, charge our phones using the sunshine and even triangulate our position with GPS. But, often, simple is best. So, at this point, we'll get back to basics to prove that, sometimes, the best things in life are *completely* free…

Make your own Coke-can stove

Disclaimer: not to be attempted by anyone under 16. Always be careful with sharp objects and naked flames. We do not take responsibility for any loss or damage whatsoever caused.

With two empty cans, and a spot of DIY, you can make your own cooker! Not a new idea – this simple stove can be traced right back to 1904 New York. (Modern-day Trangias work on similar lines).

You will need:

2 empty drink cans
1 empty can of tuna with the lid removed
A sharp knife
An awl

Directions:

1. Turn one of the drink cans upside down. Around the base rim pierce a series of 12 evenly spaced holes using the awl.

2. In the centre of the base, pierce a further three small holes with the awl.

3. Using your knife, cut the rest of the can away so that you're left with the bottom half only, so it is now about 4 cm in height.

4. Take the other can and cut it in half. Keep the bottom half only.

5. You now need to slot the section with the holes into the section without, so that the holes are facing upwards. If you have difficulty in getting them to fit, then bend the sides inwards.

6. Once they have slotted together, give them a tap to make sure they are secure. Your stove is complete!

7. To light it, place your stove with the holes facing up into the empty can of tuna. Then pour methylated spirits (available from camping/ outdoor shops) into the three holes in the centre. Stop before the liquid reaches the top of the holes. Then put a couple of drops of the meths into the tuna can.

8. Light the meths in the tuna can. This will prime the Coke-can stove, warming up the fuel inside it and forcing it to combust and exit through your 'jet holes' on the top. Get cooking!

PLEASE NOTE: To boil water will take about 12 minutes. The first time you use the stove it is best to underestimate how much fuel you might need and gradually increase it each time you do it. You can always add more fuel, but you obviously can't remove it once it's lit! This device should only be used *outside* the tent, and only by responsible adults.

Starting a fire without matches

This is the party piece of every 'bushcrafter' worth his or her salt! There's more than one way to do it, but all of them require tinder for kindling – think bark, dried grass, fir cones, pine needles, dry fungi or wood shavings.

Sunlight

What do I need? Any kind of lens – be it magnifying glass, eyeglasses or binoculars.

What do I do? Angle the lens towards the sun to focus the beam on your tinder, be patient and soon you'll get your fire.

Drawbacks: Needs good sunlight. Overcast conditions won't work.

Friction

What do I need? A piece of cord, a bendable branch, a soft wooden plank of dead, dry wood (e.g. sycamore, willow or birch), a knife, a hard wooden branch and a rock.

What do I do?

Make a bow by tying the cord to each end of the bendable wooden branch. In the soft plank – 'the fireboard' – use the hard wooden branch to drill a small depression about 2 cm from the edge. Then, using your knife, cut a V-shaped notch in the centre of the depression. Put your tinder on a leaf or similar (to keep it all together) then place this underneath the notch. Grab the hard wooden branch – your drill – and twist it into the bow, securing it between the notch in the fireboard and the rock. Then start sawing to create friction. In doing so, after persevering, embers will be created on your kindling. Pick them up and blow on them to add oxygen and you'll get your flame.

Drawbacks: It can take time to find the pieces required to build this apparatus – and it takes a fair amount of patience and practise to get this device to work.

To be on the safe side… consider carrying a fire-steel with you, as this will work to create sparks no matter what. Even if you find yourself in damp conditions, you should be able to start a fire. They're available from all good camping stores.

Making a survival shelter

Caught short without a tent? Want to make a quick makeshift shelter? Here's how.

What you need to look for:

One long straight branch - around 2.5 m long
Two shorter branches - around 1 m long each
Cord or twine (if available)
Plenty of short branches, dead leaves and grass

1. Take the two short branches and the longer straight one to form a tripod shape, secure them with cord if you have it (this can be a shoelace or string from your rucksack or even a belt in an emergency). This will form the frame for your shelter. Once erected, before going any further, check that you can fit yourself inside the frame. If you can't, then swap the sticks for longer ones and proceed to step 2.

2. Now, using the selection of smaller branches, begin to build up the walls along the longer, central pole. Pack them as close together as you can, then begin to insulate them using the dead leaves, grass, and even soil around the base to keep it secure.

3. Keep going until the frame is covered, but leaving the smallest side open.

4. Your shelter is now ready; the open end is for your head, the narrow end for your feet. You can use your rucksack to 'close' the entrance if needed.

Other ways to shelter

If you're not in a forest and trees are not abundant, there are other things you can do:

- If you're out in the open the best thing to do is keep your back to the wind. Use anything you have to insulate you from it, e.g. a rucksack.

- Boulders – use as a windbreak, or look for overhangs to squeeze into, thus giving you some protection from the elements.

- Layer up – don't forget that you should walk fully equipped to deal with bad weather, so if you have to stop due to adverse conditions, remember to put on all your warm layers and get into a sleeping bag if necessary. Many victims of hypothermia have been found with a bag still full of warm clothes that they failed to put on before they began to get confused (a classic symptom of hypothermia).

Natural remedies

Forget something in your first aid kit? Don't panic, as you might just find it's been provided for by Mother Nature herself…

Sphagnum moss: A favourite of bushcrafters, this green, peaty moss has antiseptic properties; so if you scratch yourself or get a small cut when camping, this is perfect to clean the wound – you simply rub the leaves (which will be watery) over the affected area. It's also great for cleaning out your bowls and cups. Found on boggy ground, it's soft to the touch, and can be recognised by its tiny leaves, which can be toothed, grow in tufts close to the stem and are usually light green.

Birch polypore fungi: Forgotten the blister plasters? Not to worry. These large, white fungi slabs are found in the woods, growing on rotting trees. They are shaped like shelves and always grow horizontally. They are spongy, non-toxic and contain antibiotics. Very absorbent, birch polypore fungi is naturally cooling, anti-inflammatory and antibacterial and is also easy to cut into any shape to place directly on the affected skin.

Dock leaves: One most of us probably used in childhood – but worth remembering. If you get stung by nettles look out for one of these perennial weeds which are always found nearby. The leaves contain a natural astringent that soothe. They can also be used on burns and blisters.

Find your way...

While you should always take a map and compass with you if heading into the wilds (and know how to use them properly), it can be fun to practise some tried and tested techniques to help you find North. Once you've figured that out, you can work out your position and where to go next.

Finding North at night:

You can find the Polaris (aka the North Star) using the saucepan-shaped Plough constellation.

1. First, pick out the two stars that form the vertical edge of the 'pan' furthest from the 'handle'.

2. Next, hold up your arm and line up those stars against the edge of your hand.

3. Follow the line at this angle for four times the distance between the two stars.

4. This will take you to the North Star – a very bright star. Once facing this you know you're roughly facing north, with west to your left and east to your right.

In the daytime, find South:

A good reason to remain 'analogue' with a traditional clock face on your wrist – rather than invest in the new all-singing all-dancing smart watches – is this very neat bushcraft trick.

1. Line up the hour hand on your watch so that it's pointing at the sun.

2. Draw an imaginary a line through the watch face at the midway point between the 12 and the hour hand.

3. This line will indicate which way is south; from this you can work out, north, east and west.

Look for clues

You don't always need a watch or the night sky to work out your north from your west; nature leaves clues for us – you just have to know what to look for.

If you're in the woods... Look at the trees near the edge of the tree-line. The side that faces the sun will have bark that is noticeably thinner – this will be the direction *south* if you're in the northern hemisphere. So the thicker-barked side will indicate *north*. As a general rule, trees also bend away from the prevailing wind (roughly south-west), and more branches grow on the sheltered side (north-east). So check out which way the trees seem to be leaning.

If you're on high moorland... Stick a walking pole in the ground. Put a stone at the end of the shadow it casts. Wait half an hour and mark the end of the new shadow with another stone. The line that runs between these two should run approximately east–west.

If you're on the hillside... Check around the rocks for flowers. They tend to face south as that is where they get the most sun, so have a look and see which way they're pointing.

CAMPING CRITTERS
(AND OTHER MISHAPS)

'What on earth would I do if four bears came into my camp?
Why, I would die of course. Literally s**t myself lifeless.'
BILL BRYSON, *A WALK IN THE WOODS*

Of all the outdoor activities – climbing, mountaineering, biking – the actual act of camping, consisting as it does of simply cooking and sleeping, is pretty low risk. But that doesn't mean that there are no annoyances. From those vexing ticks and midges, to the slightly more intimidating grizzly bears, they probably won't cause you any problems – but if they do…

The critter: Tick

What is it? A tiny parasite that is actually part of the spider family.

Where will I find them? All over the UK, Europe, Asia and North America, on heathland and in woodland grazed by sheep or deer. They are a real problem when wild camping.

How will I recognise them? At first glance they appear as just a tiny black dot on your skin – which is why it's often hard to know that you have one on you. But, under a microscope, they are eight-legged bugs with tiny heads and larger bodies which swell as they feed.

Why should I worry? They burrow their heads down into your skin to feed on your blood. The bite itself won't cause a problem – you won't even feel them doing it because they inject you with an anesthetic at the same time – but ticks can be carriers of the bacteria that causes Lyme disease. Though easily treatable with antibiotics if detected early on, it is difficult to diagnose and, if left ignored, can cause serious and lasting problems.

Ahhh, it bit me! Don't panic. Using a pair of straight-tipped tweezers, grip the tick as close to its jaws as possible and pull it straight out in a single motion (without twisting or turning it) – the trick is to get every part of it out in one. Various implements are available to buy to remove them safely but, if you're unsure, seek medical help.

Camping Fact

Did you know that in 2009 alone there were over 29,000 reported cases of Lyme disease in the USA? (Source: Centers for Disease Control and Prevention)

The critter: Midge

What is it? Essentially tiny biting flies, there are over 40 different known species of midges in Scotland alone. They detect you by body odour and the carbon dioxide you breathe out.

Where will I find them? Anywhere in Britain, but they are a real problem in Scotland during May to September, especially near standing water, in woodland and even on high mountains. They're more prevalent at dusk and dawn.

How will I recognise them? You will probably see the swarm clouds of little black flies coming towards you. They are tiny in size but the sting you feel as they bite you will always give them away!

Why should I worry? They can be relentless, and travel in large numbers, so you never get just one bite, but several, and they can itch and sting for days afterwards - not severely, but enough to be a nuisance and to ruin any camping trip.

Ouch, it's biting me! The one thing they can't deal with is the wind; even a gentle breeze will keep them away, so heading to higher ground can help. They also tend to be attracted to dark colours, so you can try adjusting your wardrobe. Repellents can be used, as can special midge hats with netting to protect your face, but the key is to try to avoid them in the first place. If bitten, apply some cream that contains anthistamine to help prevent swelling.

The critter: Black Widow spider

What is it? There are obviously hundreds of different types of spider out there, and while none of them (save the occasional exotic visitor!) will hurt you in the UK, camping in the USA will present more of a problem - especially the Black Widow which is found in North America.

Where will I find them? Within trees and shrubs and, sometimes, in shower blocks or warm, dry laundry areas on campsites – so be particularly careful when pitching among woods or forests anywhere in the States.

How will I recognise them? They are black in colour and are made distinctive by the red hourglass-shaped mark on their abdomen.

Why should I worry? Although very few people will die from a Black Widow bite (most at risk are children or the elderly) the consequences can be pretty nasty – muscle spasms, cramps and pain for up to seven weeks after being bitten.

Ouch, it bit me! If possible, get a photo of the critter that got you or at least remember what it looked like – then get medical attention as soon as possible. Any information you give the medics will help them work out the anti-venom you need.

Camping Fact

Mosquitoes can smell the carbon dioxide in a human's breath from over 30 m away. (Source: www.mosquitosolutions.com)

The critter: Mosquito

What is it? The bigger brother of the midge, mosquitoes are flying insects – and they are after your blood.

Where will I find them? Seemingly everywhere these days, but particularly in warmer countries and the tropics, i.e. Africa, Asia, the Caribbean, North America.

How will I recognise them? Normally you'll hear them making a high-pitched buzz as they circle you. They are usually larger than midges and have a protruding proboscis (the needle-like appendage they use to pierce skin and suck your blood).

Why should I worry? Most of the time they are just an irritation, leaving an itchy bite behind that usually heals in a few days. Though some people do get a bad reaction, the main danger is that mosquitoes can carry some really harmful infections such as malaria, dengue fever and yellow fever.

Ouch, it bit me! The best thing to do is to prevent this from happening. Wear DEET-based repellent or clothing impregnated with insect repellent. In high-risk malaria areas, consider taking antimalarials and sleep inside a mosquito net. After being bitten, use cream containing antihistamine. If you experience any flu-like symptoms post-bite and have been to a high-risk malaria country, then seek immediate medical advice.

The critter: Bear

What is it? Adorable to look at from a distance – but terrifying close-up, these large mammals come in two main types that campers need to be aware of – grizzly and black.

Where will I find them? Northern Hemisphere mainly, in mountainous and forested areas of North America, parts of Europe and Asia – particularly in autumn when they are on the hunt for food pre-hibernation.

How will I recognise them? Grizzly bears are larger, with a hump at the ruff of their neck. Black bears are smaller but don't let the name fool you – both can be a number of colours, from black to brown and even blonde.

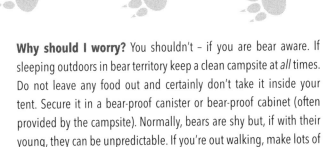

Why should I worry? You shouldn't – if you are bear aware. If sleeping outdoors in bear territory keep a clean campsite at *all* times. Do not leave any food out and certainly don't take it inside your tent. Secure it in a bear-proof canister or bear-proof cabinet (often provided by the campsite). Normally, bears are shy but, if with their young, they can be unpredictable. If you're out walking, make lots of noise – attacks usually happen because they've been surprised.

Oh no – it's charging me! Don't run. A bear can charge at around 35 mph, so you will never outrun it. In comparison, Usain Bolt – the fastest man in the world – can only reach 27 mph. Try to back away slowly and calmly, speaking softly to reassure the bear that you are not a threat. If it starts to charge, make lots of noise: clap your hands, yell, bang pots and pans and make yourself as big as possible. If it attacks, use your bear spray (if you have it); if you don't and it's a grizzly, then play dead in the foetal position, protecting your head and abdomen. If it's a black bear you have the option to fight back – use anything to hand, a walking pole, a rock, your fists – as it is less likely to give up if you play dead.

Other hazards

Critters and wildlife may be the obvious things that most campers worry about, but realistically there are other more mundane hazards that you're far more likely to have to deal with...

Cuts and bruises

In cold and wet weather, fiddling around with guy lines, banging tent pegs into tough ground or trying to sort out stubborn zips often result in the odd scrape or knock. These little events are nothing to really worry about, but remember to keep any wound clean to stop infection, and take some antibacterial wipes or cream and plasters with you, just in case.

Burns

Did you know that an average fire can reach temperatures of around 400 degrees C? Be careful around your cooking stove and campfire, and remember that you can burn yourself on the food you've take off it, and even scald your fingers if touching a metal camping mug full of boiling water. If you do burn yourself, run the burn under cool water (you could use a stream if in the wild) for five to ten minutes. A painkiller can be taken for any pain but, if it is a bad burn, seek immediate medical advice and help as shock or infection can occur.

Sunburn

It's not just your nylon tent that suffers from prolonged exposure with the sun – your skin won't like it either. Even if it's overcast you can still get burned – and all the more easily at higher altitude. So take with you – and use – suncream as well as lip balm with SPF (Sun Protection Factor) in it.

Remember, most campers' experiences are trouble-free so there really is no need to worry unnecessarily; but knowing the basics can help keep you keep calm if the worst does happen.

CHAPTER 10

CONSTANT CAMPERS

'A great many people, and more all the time, live their entire lives without ever once sleeping out under the stars.'
ALAN S. KESSELHEIM, *LET THEM PADDLE: COMING OF AGE ON THE WATER*

These days, though permanent dwellings are the order of the day for most of us, there are still some nomadic tribes left – even in our modern world – who live full-time under canvas, or even under the stars with just a mat and sleeping bag as their home. They move around the land, grazing cattle and setting up home temporarily until the resources run out. Then they simply move on.

North Africa and the Middle East

The Bedouin are one such group. They roam parts of North Africa and the Middle East, setting up camps out in the desert and travelling around regularly, with the only constant being the moon and stars in the sky above their beds. Mainly Arabic in ethnicity, they have travelled the land for centuries and are even named in the Bible. Their name comes from the Arabic word for 'nomad' or 'wanderer'. Though, nowadays, many Bedouin do tend to stay put, choosing to live in western-style houses – the village at Wadi Rum in Jordan, for example – others would never give up their nomadic heritage and continue to wander across the land.

Asia

In Asia you will find that the Steppes – an eco-region stretching across Eastern Europe and Central Asia, from Ukraine to Tian Shan – still see nomadic tribes moving across the land, searching for pastures for their livestock. Their cattle are the means to feed and clothe their families so are vital for the nomads' survival. Again, the draw of an easier way of life means that some have moved into the cities. However, in Mongolia, it is estimated that over half the population is still living nomadically. They dwell in 'gers' – what we often incorrectly call yurts (the yurt actually has its origins in Turkey) – and raise horses, cows, yaks, sheep and goats. Families tend to gather twice a year in groups, both pre-summer and pre-winter, and move to sheltered spots when the weather gets colder so that their precious cattle have the best chance of survival. Their gers are constructed using a wooden frame that is then covered in layers of felt for warmth. They are extremely good at keeping out the extreme weather conditions and usually feature a central stove. Whole families of around seven to nine people will typically share one ger, which creates a communal atmosphere and, of course, assists with maintaining heat. When the family needs to relocate, they simply dismantle the structure and take it with them – reassembling it when they find their next camp. Though it would take anyone else a lot longer, the average time for packing away a ger is an impressive two to three hours.

North America

Over in North America, though the majority of Native Americans in the USA and Inuit communities up in Arctic Canada have adopted modern houses to live in on their reservations and within their communities, they still teach their children about their nomadic past. From the teepee – the animal-skin-covered wooden frame used mainly by the tribes on the Great Plains, to the Wigwam – a bark covered dome-like structure used mainly in the north-eastern states and igloos in the Arctic north carved out of snow – they believe it to be important that their children remember the dwellings of the past. Ironically, it is now Westerners who are intrigued to experience life in these once temporary structures and who can be found on many a luxury campsite – built especially for tourists to get a fleeting glimpse of life when camping was king.

Armies, aid and protest

Of course, though fewer people live in tents now, they are still used for temporary accommodation for day-to-day living – and no more so than in the army. Recent scenes of war in parts of the Middle East see soldiers encamped in mess tents on temporary bases. Not that this military use is anything new. During their quest for world domination, the Romans were known for erecting huge camps wherever they went – using tents made of leather which were big enough to house thousands of their men. But, being Romans, they weren't just put up in a haphazard fashion – these were fancy encampments that boasted streets and a town centre, with lower ranked officers set further away from the middle. Hierarchies in army campsites may still exist today, even though leather tents do not!

Aid workers, too, often need to erect makeshift shelters following natural disasters such as hurricanes, tsunamis and earthquakes, or when helping in war-torn countries, and also in the midst of a medical crisis. Enter the tent – providing sleeping quarters, emergency accommodation and in-the-field clinics. Many aid organisations opt for box-style tents for maximum room, or dome-style designs capable of withstanding the elements.

Finally, who can forget the Occupy London protesters, camped outside St Paul's for nearly a year in 2012 – and those who joined in solidarity over on the other side of the pond in New York's Wall Street. When people are leaving their homes to go out and make a difference in the world, they need temporary accommodation so, once again, the trusty tent makes an appearance.

Longing for the past

When it comes to tents as part of everyday life it seems that we humans are reluctant to let go – look around and you'll see that echoes of our pitchable favourites abound. From marquees at weddings to actual concrete structures designed by architects, all nod to our canvas past. It seems we're not really quite ready to let go of our own nomadic roots!

Buildings inspired by tents

- London's O2 arena – With its dome-shaped design and 12 yellow poles it resembles a giant marquee in the process of being pitched.

- Denver's International Airport – A series of teepee-shaped pyramids, stretched out in a row that looks like an old Native American campground.

- Munich's Olympiastadion – designed with see-through tent-like structures all over the roof, this sports ground was meant to celebrate a new and more optimistic Germany.

So what's in a name?

When is a tent not a tent? When it's one of these appellations! So how many have you heard of?

Yurt – A wooden frame temporary tent structure used by Turks in Central Asia. Made of a lattice wall, roof ribs and flooring, all of which create traction for the main structure, they are then lined with wool or felt.

Lavvu – A tent used by the Sami of northern Scandinavia. Similar to a Chum, it's made from three tripod-like poles that are secured. Extra loose poles are then added to help shape the structure.

Kohte – A large German scouting tent used for groups. These tents are, unusually, black in colour, and are made of four heavy canvas pieces to form a triangular prism; the 'poles', made of wood, actually support it outside the canvas with the fabric hanging down below it.

Pandal – A type of fabric structure constructed for religious ceremonies in Asia. Very elaborate design – with swathes of fabric and hanging lights that often rely on trees for their structure.

Loue – A very simple, ultra-light Finnish tent designed for one or two people. It consists of just one pole and a single piece of fabric, which has a rounded and wider bottom and narrows at the top – resembling a more structured tarp.

Chum – A wigwam-type tent used by nomadic Siberian and Russian reindeer herders. More squat than a teepee, and larger than a lavvu the 'canvas' is reindeer skin and the poles are wooden, with a hole left at the top to enable a fire inside (the smoke also keeps away mosquitoes).

CHAPTER 11

HALL OF FAME

*'For as long as I stay here, I know I will have
to also get to the wild places.'*
ROBERT MACFARLANE

It's not just the founder of The Camping and Caravanning Club,
Thomas Hiram Holding, whose name you should know. When it
comes to sleeping under canvas, heading to wild places and falling
in love with the great outdoors, we have several other people who
championed – and are still backing – the camping cause.

Henry Hopkins Sibley (1816-1886)

Created a tent used by the army

To gear fans, this American brigadier's name may already have the ring of familiarity about it. Though military enthusiasts will be familiar with him for his work in the Civil War, we outdoor lovers know him for one reason and one reason only – the Sibley Tent. A conical design, and similar to the tents used by the Native Americans, it was held in place by tent pegs and no guy lines, simply using a central pole and tripod stand. This enabled a stove for cooking and heating to be placed inside. Using a vent with a loose covering over it, smoke could get out, but rain couldn't get in. Sibley patented his design in 1856 and it went on to be used in the American Civil War and also in World War Two. He was supposed to receive the princely sum of $5 per tent constructed from his design, but never saw a penny after he resigned from the US Army to join the Confederate States side! So, when glamping, if you happen to see a bell tent or a teepee, spare a thought for one Henry Sibley. We salute you, Sir!

Henry David Thoreau (1817-1862)

American author, poet and philosopher, who showed us we could all go back to basics

Though a philosopher, abolitionist and top transcendentalist, most of us will be more familiar with Thoreau's seminal text – *Walden; or, Life in the Woods* – than with the man himself. Indeed, it is for that reason that he makes this list. Thoreau's book documents his mission to strip his life of all complications and reconnect with nature – and with himself. In 1845, he began this quest. For two years, two weeks and two days he lived in a tiny hut on the edge of Walden Pond. It wasn't that he'd truly gone into the wild – the structure was only a couple of kilometres from his family home – but he had built it himself and had grown his own food in an attempt to be as self-sufficient as possible. The longer he stayed, the more he waxed lyrical about the nature that surrounded him and the beauty of the natural world. With revelations that the only medicine he needed was 'a draught of morning air' and his assertions that the wild was somewhere to be loved and cherished if mankind is ever to find true happiness, we become lost in his journey. Through his meetings with others, and his ramblings in the forest, he deconstructs the American dream and considers whether the quest for money and possessions is really worth it. It may not have been a tent he stayed in, but read this wonderful book and you will understand a little more why we are, and always will be, attracted to sleeping in the simplest of structures, surrounded by nature.

Anna 'Nan' Shepherd (1893-1981)

Made the mountains and landscapes of Scotland come alive even after her death

Rammed full of vivid descriptions of the Cairngorms, and long before nature writing became 'trendy', Nan's books allowed the humanist nature of the hills to dominate most of her novels and poems. By far the most influential work for hill-goers and wild campers is *The Living Mountain*, which was written during the 1940s, but only published in 1977, four years before she died. Writing on a subject that was then dominated by men who 'conquered' hills and 'named and claimed' crags, her work stands out, for she was not trying to overcome the wild but, rather, merge with it. She saw it as an extension of herself, something she needed in order to exist, and somewhere to lose oneself in exploration rather than achieve a set goal. A wild camper before the term properly existed, she is an inspiration to us all.

Don Whillans (1933–1985)

Climber and inventor of one of the best-known expedition tents

Whillans had many achievements to his name – not least that he brought the formerly rich-man's game of mountaineering to the working classes with his determined attitude and straight-talking manner. But, as well as having a natural skill on rock, he also had a real interest in kit. It was while climbing in 1963 that he designed and constructed what is commonly referred to as the 'Whillans Box'. Rectangular and cumbersome looking, this tent actually played a crucial role in his success on overseas expeditions. Though it looked odd beside the more modern dome tents, it could stand up to severe levels of wind and snow which could destroy more conventional mountain tents, and is clearly the inspiration behind many of the large family tents still used today.

Robert 'Bob' Gillis (1948-)

Inventor of the geodesic tent

There are many tent styles out there today, but the ones that have really stood the test of time are the Geodesic variety. Popular on expeditions, at festivals and even - more recently - as emergency shelters for survivors of the 2010 Haiti earthquake, this tent's freestanding structure means that it is easy to move and remains sturdy against the elements. But it nearly didn't happen at all. Bob had tinkered around with his design, crafting his own clips from plastic, wood and rubber for quite a while before he took it to manufacturers. He made a point of living in his constructions so he could iron out any problems and be certain he was onto something. Three manufacturers rejected it, and it seemed as if the tent would never grace the pitches of the campsites across the world, but then one - The North Face - licensed it and, in 1976, The Oval Intention hit the market as the first geodesic backpacking tent ever made - and the rest, as they say, is history.

Bill Bryson (1951–)

Made us realise that there is no shame in worrying about bears when camping

Anyone who can make you squawk with laughter at the same time as describing the very real dangers of encountering a bear when under canvas in North America is alright by us! Famed for his observations on British life in *Notes from a Small Island*, it's his later book – *A Walk in the Woods* – where we see him ditch B&Bs for tents in an attempt to walk the Appalachian Trail. Overwhelmed by all the choice in gear shops, we join him as he learns all about tents, accessories and the aforementioned bears. He may not make the whole long distance walk, and without spoiling the ending I can assure you he *doesn't* get eaten by a bear, but he does make us laugh, cry and inspire us to follow in his camping footsteps, always maintaining a sense of humour along the way.

Ray Mears (1964–)

The man who brought bushcraft into our homes

Nowadays it's hard to imagine watching a TV show about bushcraft without it being presented by Ray Mears. Since he hit the screens with *Tracks* in 1994, he has become the face of survival shows, highlighting a human being's ability to live off the land and adapt to any extreme environment. Championing native peoples and their traditions – which see them living in harmony with nature rather than changing it – as well as sleeping under tarp and in self-built shelters to watch wildlife (which, he famously convinces us, lies on own shores as well as overseas), Ray made us all want to head down to our nearest patch of woodland and sleep in a makeshift tent. He made searching for wild food look possible even for we mere mortals, and inspired the next generation to learn. He teaches us that, even in this day and age of modern conveniences, we are all capable of surviving in the natural world.

Louise Wener (1966–)

A Britpop star that proved camping could be cool

Music fans will remember Ms Wener for chirpy Indie-rock songs rather than camping. Front-woman of *Sleeper* – a band that reached the height of their fame in the mid-nineties when Oasis and Blur were the flavour of the month and a fusion of guitars and catchy beats filled the charts. However, as the teens matured and a new generation of music lovers came onto the scene, *Spice Girls* and other manufactured five-pieces dominated instead. Louise Wener ditched the band and began writing – and, it seems, camping. Aside from her novels about life in rock and roll, since 2012 she has been a columnist at *Camping* magazine, showing the world that camping isn't just for ramblers and the un-cool and proving that heading for a night in a tent could appeal to VIPs too!

Cheryl Strayed (1968-)

Showed how a proper camping adventure can make for a transformative experience

It may have been drug addiction, family loss and a divorce that made her hit the wilderness trail with tent in tow – rather than a love for the outdoors – but Cheryl showed America, and indeed the world, the transformative nature of staying in the cocoon of a tent and setting herself a challenge that she would see right through to the end. Her bestselling book, *Wild: From Lost to Found on the Pacific Crest Trail*, sees her undertake the 1,100-mile hike from the Mojave Desert to the Washington border, and change and grow as a person as she does so. Not only did her book inspire women to realise that long-distance hiking was safe for solo females, but it has been made into a Hollywood movie that will hopefully inspire a whole new generation of women to grab a tent and get outside.

> *'I loved the dim, clammy dark of my tent, the cosy familiarity of the way I arranged my few belongings all around me each night.'*

Robert Macfarlane (1976-)

Showed us it's OK to ditch the tent

While he certainly wasn't the first person to realise that sleeping out under the stars without a tent above you was the ultimate camping experience, Macfarlane was the one who managed to tell the most people all about it in his bestselling book, *Wild Places*. Guiding us through history – both human and geological – he teaches us to look beneath the surface of our own countryside, showing us that discovering what's *outside* ourselves will teach us more about what's *inside*. Read *Wild Places* and you will be tempted to ditch the tent altogether...

Camping Fact

In 2014, campers were asked who would be their ideal camping companion.

The result?

Women overwhelmingly chose Bear Grylls.
Men were undecided between David Attenborough and Ray Mears.

(Source: Go Outdoors Camping Survey, 2014)

CHAPTER 12

CAMPING IN FILM AND LITERATURE

'I would rather wake up in the middle of nowhere than in any city on earth.'

STEVE MCQUEEN

Since the early 90s, when 'glamping' made its first appearance, camping has undergone something of a makeover. With celebs 'admitting' to secretly enjoying the activity and adventurers appearing on our televisions telling us how hip it is to sleep under canvas, it's starting to break free of its un-cool reputation.

Ten camping films

Still need to convince some friends? Try toasted marshmallows and a night in with any one of these ten movies, where camping is definitely the star of the show...

Carry on Camping (1969)

Who can forget Sid James' naughty cackle as a young Barbara Windsor's tiny yellow bikini shot off during her exercises at Paradise Campsite in rural England?! Filmed mainly in Buckinghamshire – and in autumn (it started in October with filming wrapping in November) – this film catapulted camping capers into the mass consciousness. With old-style A-frame tents (and other retro gear you can laugh at as you spot it), pitching mishaps, and Peeping Toms by the shower blocks, it's a roaring romp of double entendres and classic British slapstick at its best. An absolute camping classic.

Stand by Me (1986)

Based on a short novella by horror legend Stephen King (called *The Body*), the film is more a 'coming-of-age' tale rather than one with a focus on the sinister. Four friends, each with problems in their lives, embark on a mission to find the dead body of a missing boy from their town. To get to its location they undertake a long walk across train tracks and through woodland, where they must camp out in swag bags under the trees. In typical childhood fashion they tell stories and eat food around the campfire, enjoying their last moments of innocence before they are forced into maturity during a confrontation with a bully. An absolute must-see, this film shows how heading into the wild can cause inner transformation and trigger the forging of friendships that will last a lifetime.

Parent Trap (1998)

OK, this may be a film primarily about identical twins separated at birth who are trying to get their parents back together, so saving their father from marrying a horrible would-be stepmother, and you might not be overly impressed with all the cheesy hi-jinks that get them there, but consider this – they first meet each other at Summer Camp, while trying a range of fun outdoor activities, and it's another camping trip with their dad that finally makes him realise the error of his ways. It may be a little predictable because – *spoiler alert* – they all live happily ever after, but this provides cast-iron proof that camping can bring families together!

The Blair Witch Project (1999)

Of all the films listed here, this one is highly unlikely to make you want to camp – and certainly not wild camp – for the first time, so don't show it to someone who is already hesitant! But it did bring tent-bound adventures to the big screen when released in the late nineties. Set up as a 'found' collection of documentary footage discovered after three filmmakers went missing in woods in Maryland, it plays out their fateful journey to try to discover the Blair Witch (who was supposedly responsible for several murders in the area in previous years). What follows is a lot of hiking among autumn trees and a catalogue of errors from these would-be witch-hunters – including continuing to walk on even when they think they are lost, throwing away their map and clearly not bringing a sturdy enough tent to stand up to the rigours of a scare from a possible ghoul! Gripping rather than inspiring stuff, this one's definitely for initiated wild campers only!

Without a Paddle (2004)

When three friends – inseparable as children but flung apart as adults – meet up years later at a funeral, they start to question whether or not they have lived life to the fullest, as their recently departed pal did. Looking over the plans they made in their youth, they decide that the only way to have a proper adventure is to get a kayak and head into the wilderness, camping out under the stars. Of course things don't exactly go according to plan. With an over-maternal grizzly bear showing up, a couple of gun-loving rednecks on their trail, and the loss of their kit when they hit a waterfall, this is a 'when camping goes wrong' type of narrative, but with often hilarious results.

Into the Wild (2007)

Telling the true story of Christopher McCandless, this film shows how a life spent camping and living in the wild can go from happiness to hell *very* quickly. McCandless turned down an education and gave away all his money for a nomadic life. He explored the States by hitchhiking and freight-training around the country, sleeping in tents or whatever other shelter he could find. His ultimate goal was to spend months living off the land in Denali National Park, Alaska. We follow his two-year nomadic journey to arrive there, and then witness how what begins as a true wilderness adventure (he sleeps in an abandoned school bus, hunting and fishing for food) becomes an act of self-discovery, and the ultimate realisation that being surrounded by people – and friends – is actually what life is all about.

Harry Potter: The Deathly Hallows: Part One (2010)

The wizard boy, who would be the chosen one to defeat 'He Who Shall Not Be Named', grows up and leaves home in this, the seventh instalment of the film franchise. But it's not a rosy affair. Driven away from friends and family, he and his two best friends take to wild camping their way around Britain in a magical 'glamping' structure that neatly zaps itself away into Hermione's handbag. They pitch up on top of the dramatic rocks of Malham Cove in Yorkshire, enjoy a woodland camp in the Forest of Dean and tent-side views of the mountains in Glen Etive, Scotland. So, if you're toying with the idea of wild camping, this film will have you convinced to try it. You won't need a wand to be taken under its spell!

Moonrise Kingdom (2012)

Continuing on the children's movie theme is this newer release that sees camping – and finding a private idyll in the wild – as the central premise. Two young pen pals hatch a plan to meet at neighbouring summer camps and then run away to a nearby island, where they discover a perfect cove that they name the eponymous Moonrise Kingdom. They hike and swim and camp in an old A-frame tent and, as they do, fall gradually in love against the backdrop of their coastal idyll. As much as it is about relationships and the innocence of love between childhood friends, it would not have quite the same effect without the beautiful setting… and, of course, the tent!

Kings of Summer (2013)

Not so much of a tent than a full-on house, the Kings of Summer film is another coming-of-age tale where three teenagers, on the verge of adulthood, decide to free themselves of the shackles of living at home with parents and, instead, go into a clearing in the woods to build themselves their own shelter. Ramshackle and without mod cons, electrics and flushing loos, it is a simple life for the boys, and they learn to be somewhat self-sufficient, attempting to forage for food and fish (though often nipping to the nearby fast-food place!), swimming and washing in the stream and learning to set – and live by – their own rules. Things inevitably go wrong but, at the times when they do find harmony living off grid, it will make you want to grab your bivvy and head for the outdoors.

Tracks (2013)

Back in 1977, a woman called Robyn Davidson set off from Alice Springs in Australia's Northern Territory to cross the Australia Desert on foot. Armed with four camels to carry her supplies, a map, a compass and her dog, she headed off on the 1,700-mile trek by herself. As she went she slept out in a swag, using a tarp to cover herself from the sun during the day and often sleeping under the stars at night. She relied on kindness and help from an Aboriginal elder to source water at one point along the way, and also discovered what it meant to be truly alone. Her story captured everyone's imagination when it appeared in National Geographic magazine. Later, she wrote a book of the same name, which was eventually made into this film. An incredible story of a truly pioneering wild camper.

Ten camping books

Wild by Cheryl Strayed

The story of the author who, following her mother's death, a divorce, and a period of drug abuse, undertakes a 1,100 mile-hike on America's famous Pacific Crest Trail. We follow her as she heads into the wild, with her tent, in order to find herself. It's obviously a physical challenge for her, but emotionally and mentally draining, too – especially for someone who, when she started, had no backpacking experience whatsoever.

The Tent, The Bucket and Me by Emma Kennedy

A hilariously funny memoir about one woman's experiences of family camping holidays when growing up in the 1970s. Battling gale-force winds in Wales, being crammed into the back of the car with her granny, and having nothing more than a bucket as 'facilities', it's a delightful trip down memory lane for those of us who were forced to have fun in tents by our parents!

Three Men in a Boat by Jerome K. Jerome

Though originally meant to be a straight travel guide, this is now a classic travel narrative. Recounting the tales of the author and his two friends as they navigate the Thames in a camping skiff, it's crammed full of tales of misadventure, bad weather and boating difficulties. It may be old – published in 1889 – but the humour is as relevant today as it was over a hundred years ago.

To Build a Fire by Jack London

Another older title – but *definitely* a classic. This short story is one of the earliest forms of a 'man versus nature' tale, which sees the protagonist battle to survive in the Yukon against snow, ice and freezing temperatures. There are two versions of the story, with two different endings – read them both…

Swallows and Amazons by Arthur Ransome

Set in the folds of the Lake District's fells and tarns, the tales of the Walker children will help any hardened camper to remember why they love camping so much. Follow their adventures as they pitch on islands, sail dinghies and drink 'grog' (ginger beer and lemonade). Great for campers of all ages.

Extreme Sleeps by **Phoebe Smith**

Desperate for an adventure after a couple of years spent travelling, the author decides to find it in her own backyard – armed with nothing more than her trusty tent. But she shuns campsites and, instead, tries her hand at wild camping. Bedding down among the wreckage of a World War Two bomber in the Peak District, sleeping on the sand in Scotland, she takes us along with her on her journey from mild to wild camper. The sequel *Wild Nights: Camping Britain's Extremes* is also worth a look.

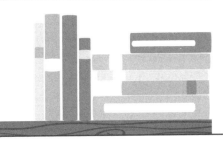

The Wild Places by **Robert Macfarlane**

Split into terrains – island, valley, mountain and moor – Macfarlane takes us on a journey to discover the wilderness spots still remaining in Britain. Combining first-person narrative with ethereal descriptions, historical accounts, and theories about what it really means for a place to be 'wild', we are taken around the country and we learn, as he does, to appreciate these great places and the fascinating stories they tell.

Cool Camping series published by Punk Publishing

If you're a campsite camper through and through then you can't go wrong with any one of the selection of guidebooks in this series. Offering a choice of England, Wales, Scotland and France in their collection, they list the very best campsites available – and a few alternatives if they are full. It will save you hours trawling the internet for a good pitch.

Wilderness Weekends by Phoebe Smith

If you want to try wild camping for yourself but don't know where to start, then this is the book for you. With expert 'how to' advice on finding wild places, as well as 26 weekends of guaranteed adventure, it also features maps and step-by-step instructions on discovering your own perfect bolthole – whether it be cave, mountaintop camp or bivvy.

No Fixed Abode by Charlie Carroll

A camping tale with a twist. In the summer of 2011, the author decided to undertake a journey on foot from Cornwall to London as a tramp, sleeping rough – urban camping if you will. Through the narrative we not only see what it's like to live in a permanent state of wild sleeping but are also forced to ask more questions about our society and its policies that, normally, we find easier to ignore.

CONCLUSION

'When it rains, look for rainbows; when it's dark, look for stars.'
ANONYMOUS

As inspiring as other people's books, films and adventures are for the days when you're back in the permanent structure of your office or home, it's those camping experiences – *your* camping experiences that you've actually had, that you are still yet to have and that you one day dream of having – that are the most exciting.

By reading this book you can become equipped with the knowledge to camp smarter, to pack your kit better and to deal with critters (including your own children weather-bound in a tent) more confidently. You can work out where to take your tent, be able to spot a lavvu or chum at fifty paces and even make a camping stove from two soda cans. But above all these things, you should now realise that though camping might not change your life, it can certainly bring joy to it, in more ways than you could ever imagine; whether it's from watching the clouds clear after a storm, from snuggling warm in your sleeping bag while the rain hammers down on your tent walls, or from that special moment when night falls and you emerge from your canvas cocoon for a dash to the toilet, catch a glimpse of the millions of stars that twinkle above us and realise that, though they are always there, you never took the time to appreciate them before.

As the late, great, nature writer Roger Deakin once said, though we are attracted to the permanence that houses made of bricks and mortar offer us: 'A camp represents the true reality of things: we're just passing through.' So make sure you pass through in style, whether pitched in a campsite, wild on a mountainside, with all the latest technology to guide you or with nothing more than nature as your compass.

It doesn't matter how you camp – just camp, and when it rains, which it will always inevitably do, remember to smile like you did when you were a child playing in your pillow-built fort. The whole world is out there, a new adventure waits at sunrise and you in your tent are one step closer to it than everyone else.

THE JOY OF WALKING

DAVID BATHURST

THE JOY OF WALKING

David Bathurst

ISBN: 978 1 84953 553 3   Hardback   £9.99

An early-morning walk is a blessing for the whole day.
HENRY DAVID THOREAU

This pocket-sized miscellany, packed with fascinating facts, handy hints and captivating stories from the world of walking, is perfect for anyone who knows the incomparable joy and freedom of lacing up their hiking boots and heading for the hills.